Dorie Hruska

Making Connections

A Free-Motion Quilting Workbook

12 Design Suites
For Longarm or Domestic Machines

C&T PUBLISHING

Text copyright
© 2017 by Dorie Hruska

Photography, and
artwork copyright © 2017
by C&T Publishing, Inc.

Publisher:
Amy Marson

Creative Director:
Gailen Runge

Editors:
Donna di Natale and
Liz Aneloski

Technical Editor:
Linda Johnson

Cover/Book Designer:
April Mostek

Production Coordinator:
Tim Manibusan

Production Editor:
Jennifer Warren

Illustrator:
Valyrie Gillum

Photo Assistant:
Mai Yong Vang

Instructional photography
by Diane Pedersen
of C&T Publishing, Inc.,
unless otherwise noted

Published by C&T Publishing, Inc., P.O. Box 1456, Lafayette, CA 94549

Printed in China

10 9 8 7 6 5 4 3 2 1

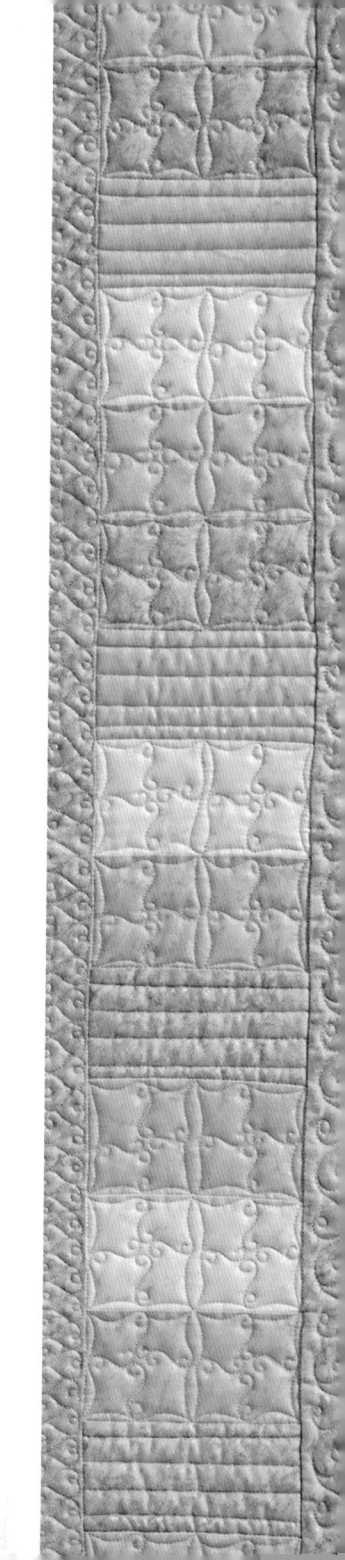

Contents

Dedication

*To my mother, Marsha, who taught me
the love of being creative*

Introduction

Quilters have been stitching continuous curved designs for years and calling them all kinds of different names. In this workbook, we will be looking at many different variations of these designs and expanding upon them, providing limitless possibilities for quilting. To take it a step further, we'll travel into open spaces like borders and large triangles, filling them in with these connecting designs. We will also look at applying this concept to the entire quilt top.

Time is a precious thing. You can spend your time stitching individual motifs in each area of a quilt, stopping and cutting your threads after each design, or you can save time by connecting the designs—stitching them from one side of the quilt all the way to the other side, with just one start and stop. By keeping the designs simple, you can achieve a more complicated look. By repeating those designs throughout the quilt, you can also create a balance in design and texture.

Making Connections—A Free-Motion Quilting Workbook is a collection of custom quilting designs for fewer starts and stops, including step-by-step instructions on how to get started. As you work through this book, I hope you will discover just how easy it is to quilt these designs and maybe come up with a few of your own.

Forever quilting,

Dorie

Objectives for This Book

- Learn how to use connecting designs to connect stitching lines with fewer stops and starts.

- Complete the quilting faster by using freehand designs (versus ruler work).

- Limit or eliminate stitch-in-the-ditch quilting.

How to Use This Book

In this workbook, basic concepts and stitching designs are introduced first in straightforward squares and squares on point. As the study continues, we will develop a skill set of more difficult designs and filler motifs. Armed with an arsenal of designs, we will then focus on continuous-line strategies within more complicated, irregular blocks. After a quilt top is pieced using the pattern included, all of these skills will be put to use in a final project. The last chapter provides instruction on the execution of continuous-line quilting, from sashing to blocks, setting triangles, corners, and borders.

The following is a color key of stitching lines used for instructional purposes:

- **Blue:** first pass
- **Green:** second pass
- **Orange:** third pass
- **Purple:** fourth pass
- **Single red dots:** intersections
- **Solid red lines:** exit paths
- **Dashed red lines:** travel paths
- **Dotted red lines:** secondary travel paths

Practice Drawing

Let's begin practicing by drawing the designs in rows.

For the first very basic stitching design, start drawing from the top left corner and work to the right along the top edge.

Start

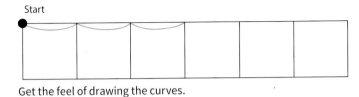

Get the feel of drawing the curves.

Now let's move on.

Say to yourself, "Over, down, up … over, down, up … " until you finish the row.

Start

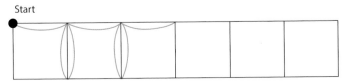

First line of a very basic stitching design

To finish the design, draw a second line from right to left: Over • Over • Over, to the end of the row.

Start

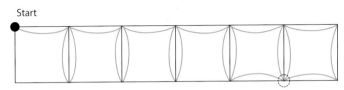

Second line to finish the design

....
Tip • Every time you come into the corners, aim for the intersection.
....

Once you feel comfortable, you can progress to practicing the full design in a block.

Train yourself to execute these designs in an overall *clockwise* direction. Part of the design might include going from right to left and left to right, but the overall progression will be clockwise as you move around the area.

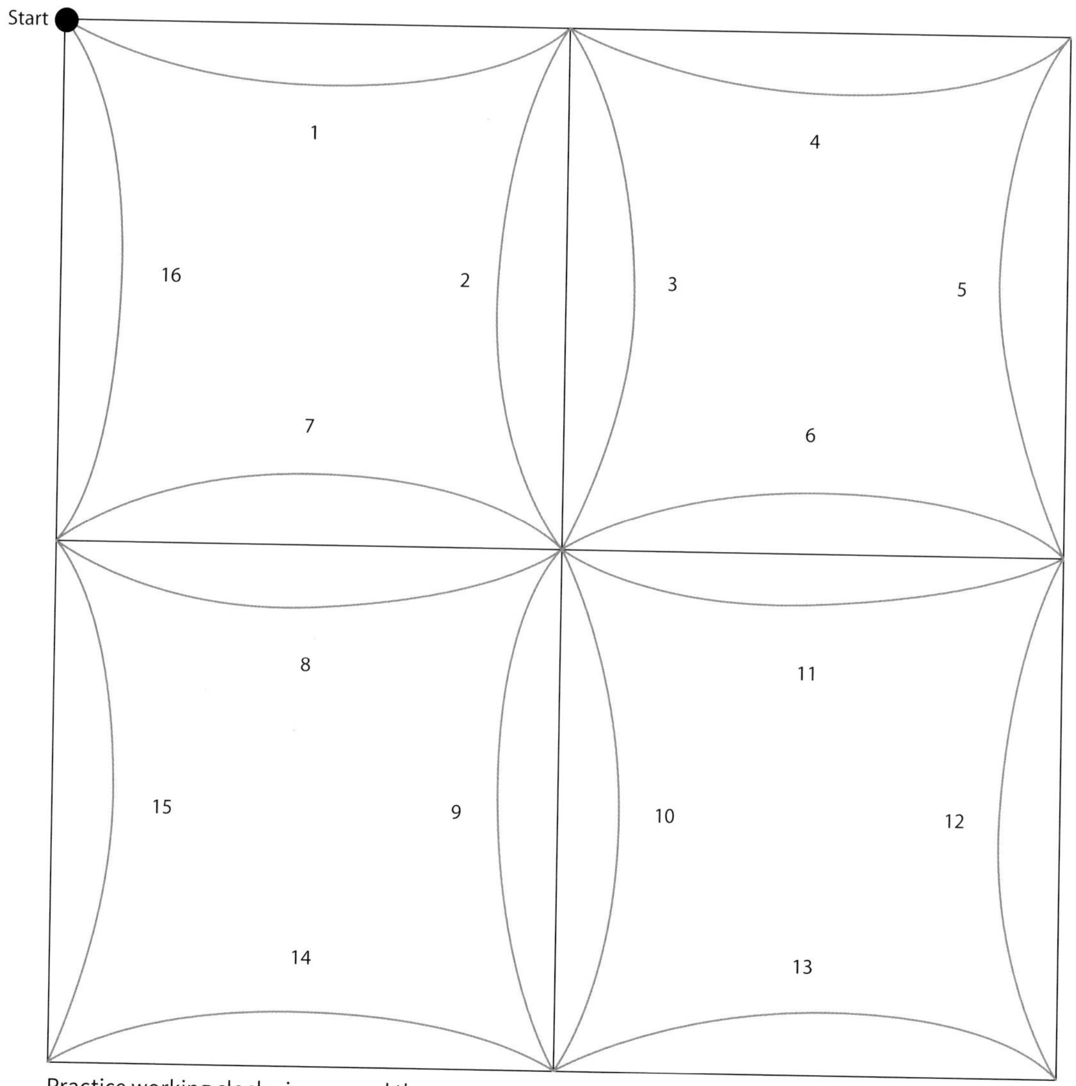

Start

1

16   2   3   5

7   6

8   11

15   9   10   12

14   13

Practice working clockwise around the area.

Follow the numbering system for each design. By practicing in this manner, you will be able to master the flow of a basic symmetrical block.

In each design section of this book, you will be given illustrations for stitching the design in a four-patch layout (basic squares) and in two border-and-corner grids (squares on point), plus a blank worksheet on which to practice drawing.

Borders and Sashing—Basic Information

Consider the width of the border or sashing when choosing a design. If your space is small, a simple design is all you need. But if you have a larger (wider) space to fill or you want the area more densely quilted, you may want to consider a double design with extra fillers.

No matter which design you choose, be sure to keep the amount of quilting balanced throughout the quilt so it lies nice and flat.

Stitching inside the grid plus adding a filler—1 pass

Stitching inside and outside the grid—2 passes

Start

Stitching a fuller design inside, stitching the outside, and adding an outline—3 passes

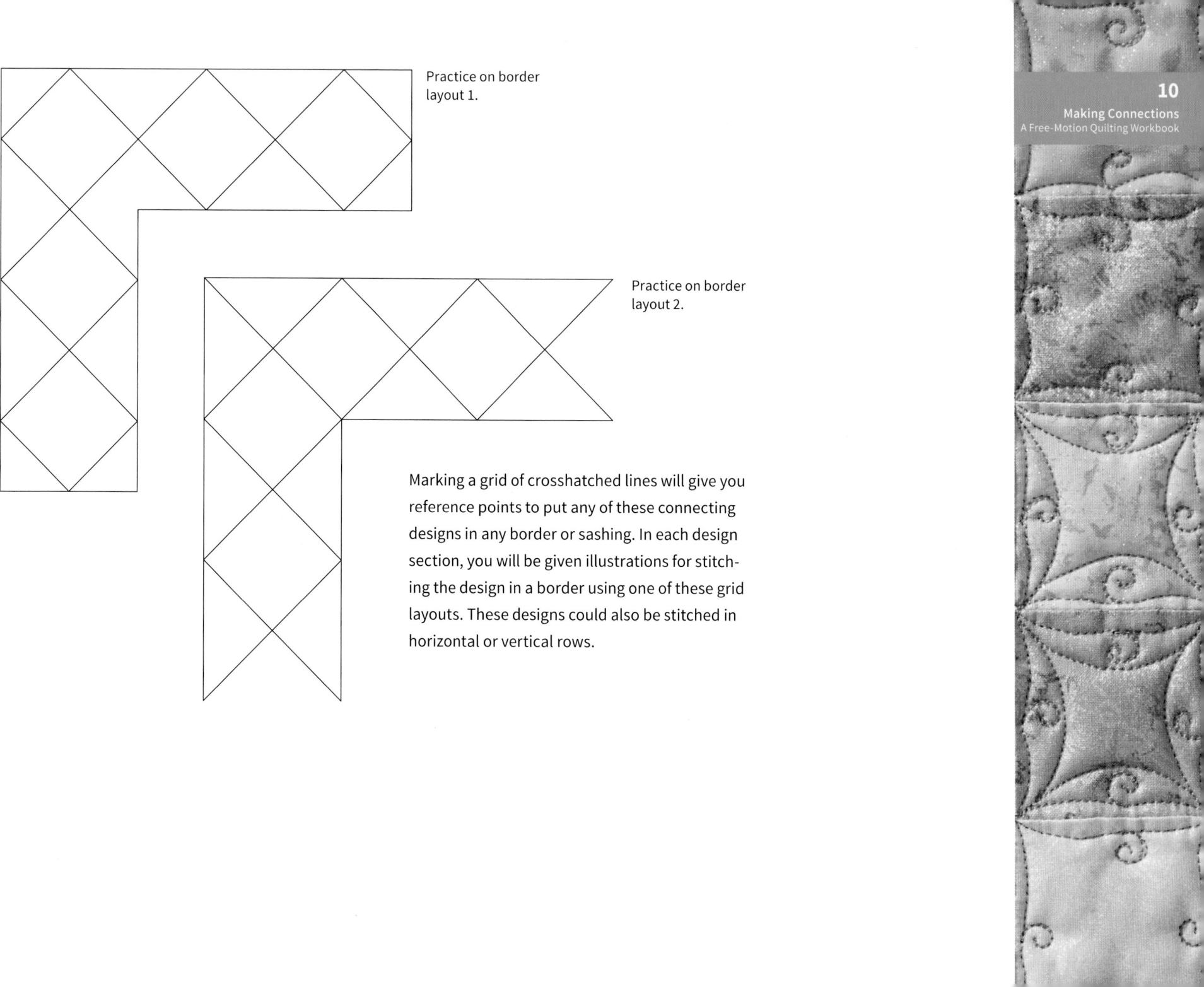

Practice on border layout 1.

Practice on border layout 2.

Marking a grid of crosshatched lines will give you reference points to put any of these connecting designs in any border or sashing. In each design section, you will be given illustrations for stitching the design in a border using one of these grid layouts. These designs could also be stitched in horizontal or vertical rows.

To make these steps even easier, I have designed a set of square grid stencils that are measured on the diagonal. They come in 1″, 2″, or 3″ widths and are available for purchase on my website, Forever Quilting (forever-quilting.com). In conjunction with my stencils, Miracle Chalk is my go-to company for quilt-marking products. Their pounce pad, the Quick Swipe marking pad, is especially easy to use. A tap of a hot iron erases the lines entirely.

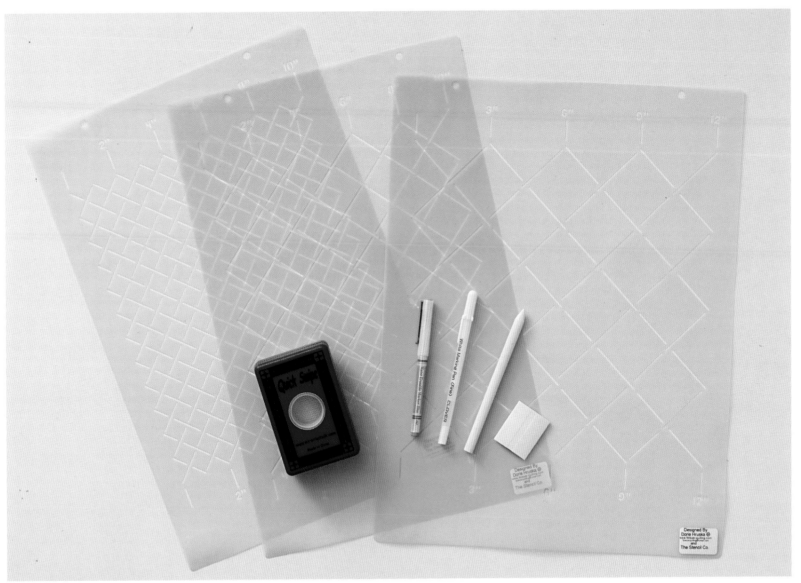

Stencils and marking tools

For example, a border strip may be cut 6½″ wide. You could use any of these stencils to mark a 1″, 2″, or 3″ grid on your 6″ finished border, because 6 is divisible by 1, 2, and 3.

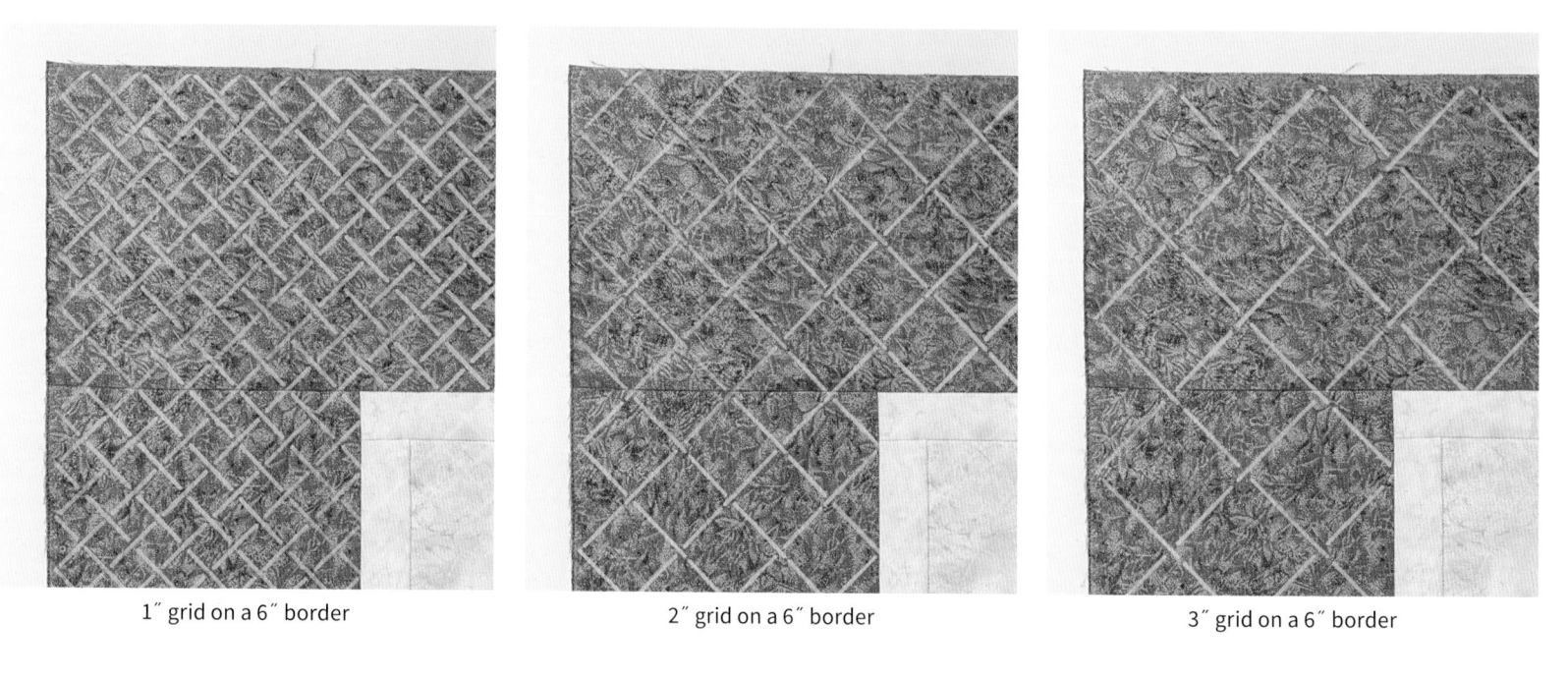

1″ grid on a 6″ border   2″ grid on a 6″ border   3″ grid on a 6″ border

In these examples, the borders are marked with an on-point grid using a stencil and pounce pad. These lines will be removed after the quilting is complete. You can use any of your favorite marking tools or utilize the seamlines of your pieced blocks as your reference points.

Stenciled grid

Quilt inside the grid and travel through the squares.

Complete the stitching inside the grid.

Stitch outside the grid.

Complete the stitching outside the grid.

Note

If this is an outside border, you will need to keep the design ¼″ away from the outside edge to allow for the binding. You do not want to cut off or cover up part of the design when you attach your binding.

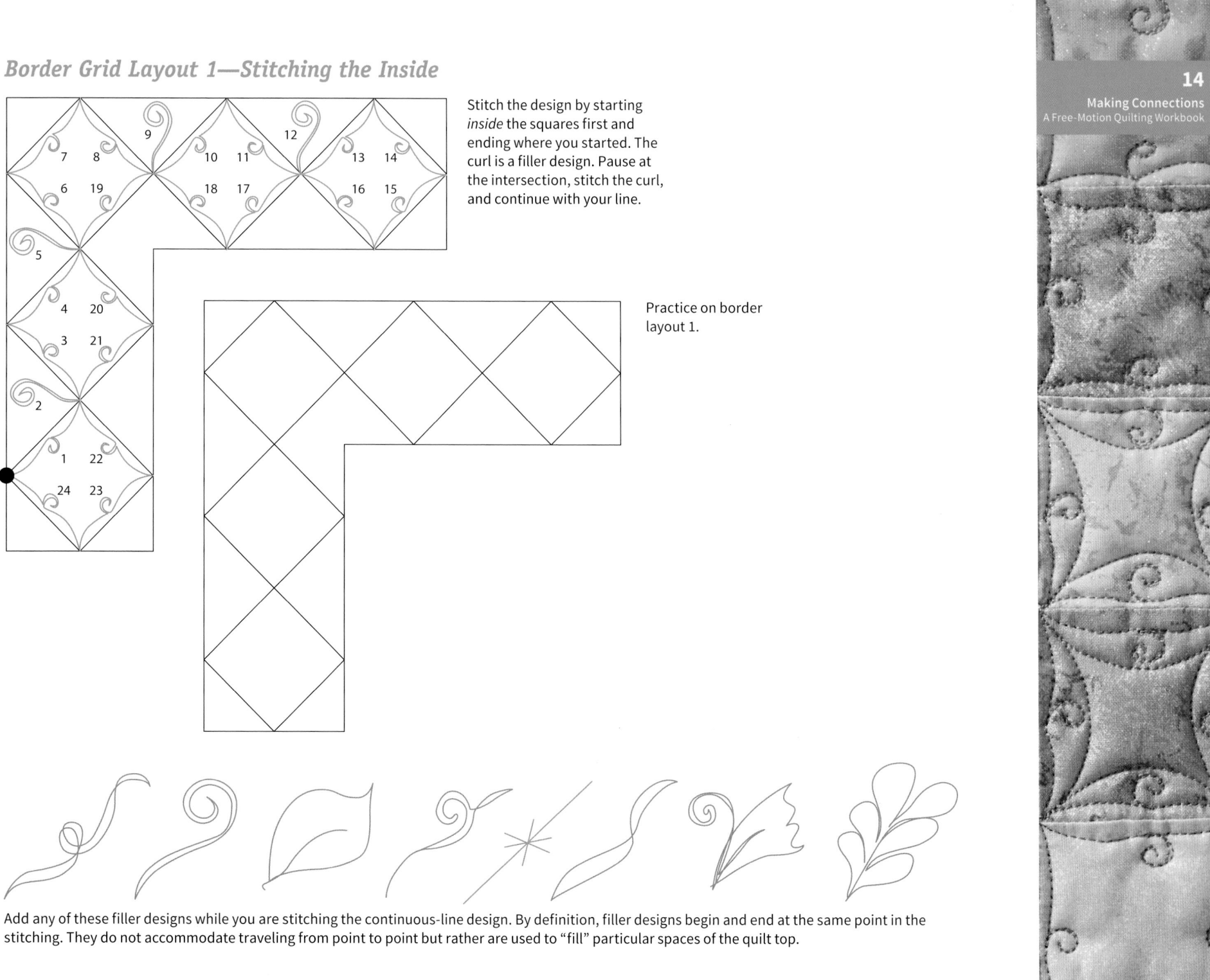

Border Grid Layout 1—Stitching the Inside

Stitch the design by starting *inside* the squares first and ending where you started. The curl is a filler design. Pause at the intersection, stitch the curl, and continue with your line.

Practice on border layout 1.

Add any of these filler designs while you are stitching the continuous-line design. By definition, filler designs begin and end at the same point in the stitching. They do not accommodate traveling from point to point but rather are used to "fill" particular spaces of the quilt top.

Border Grid Layout 1—Stitching the Outside

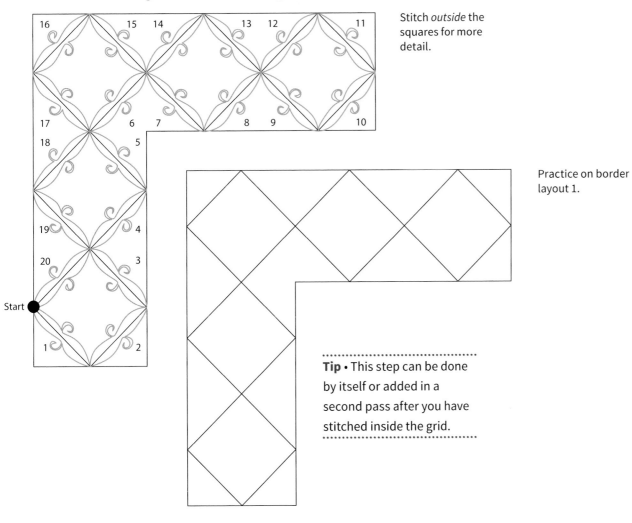

Stitch *outside* the squares for more detail.

Practice on border layout 1.

Tip • This step can be done by itself or added in a second pass after you have stitched inside the grid.

Border Grid Layout 2—Stitching the Inside

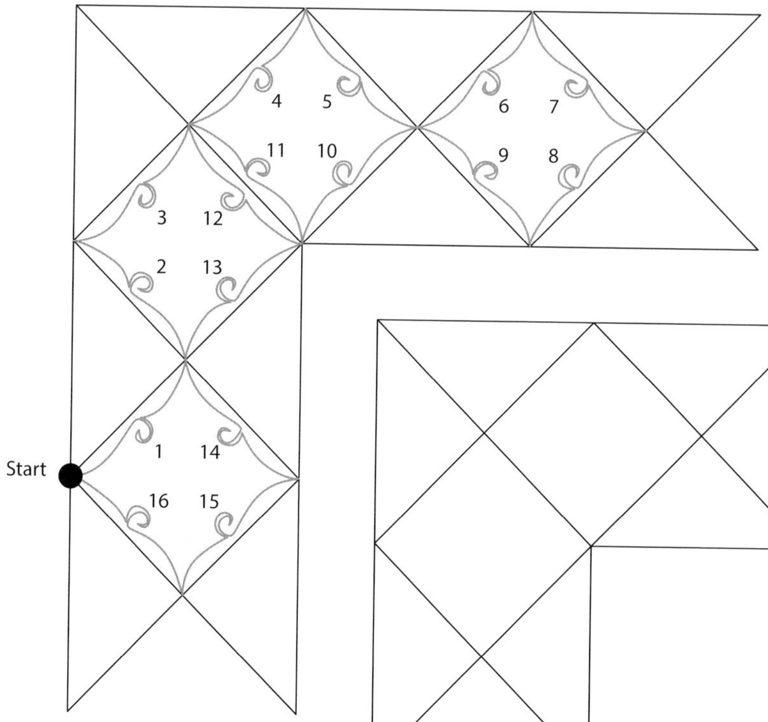

Stitch the design by starting *inside* the squares first and ending where you started.

Practice on border layout 2.

Start

Border Grid Layout 2—Stitching the Outside

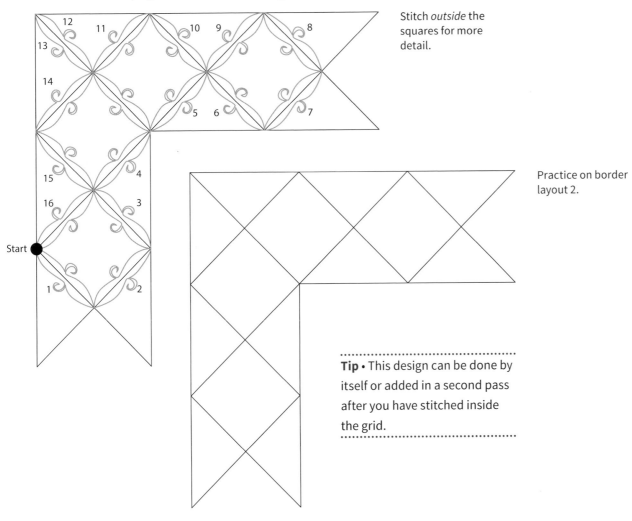

Stitch *outside* the squares for more detail.

Practice on border layout 2.

Tip • This design can be done by itself or added in a second pass after you have stitched inside the grid.

FOUR-PATCH LAYOUT

Follow the numbered sequence. The red lines are stitched last; they are your exit path.

···

Tip • Master the flow of this basic connecting design. It is repeated throughout this book.

···

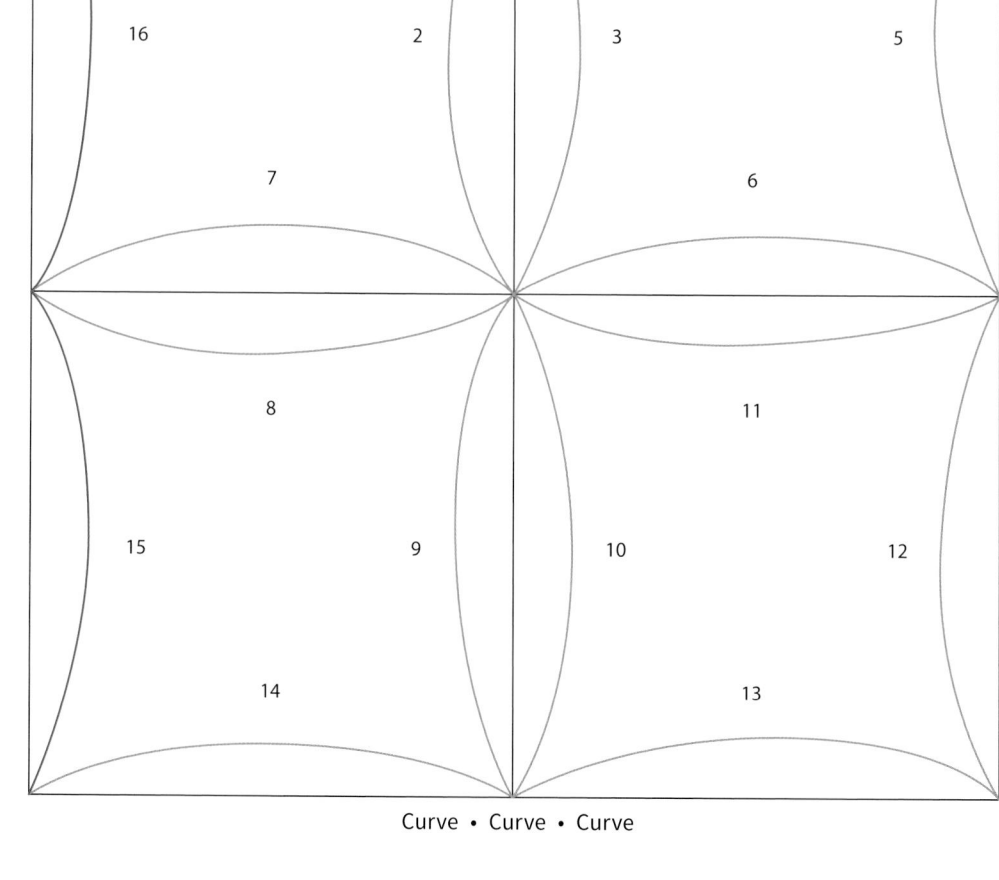

Start

1	4
16 2	3 5
7	6
8	11
15 9	10 12
14	13

Curve • Curve • Curve

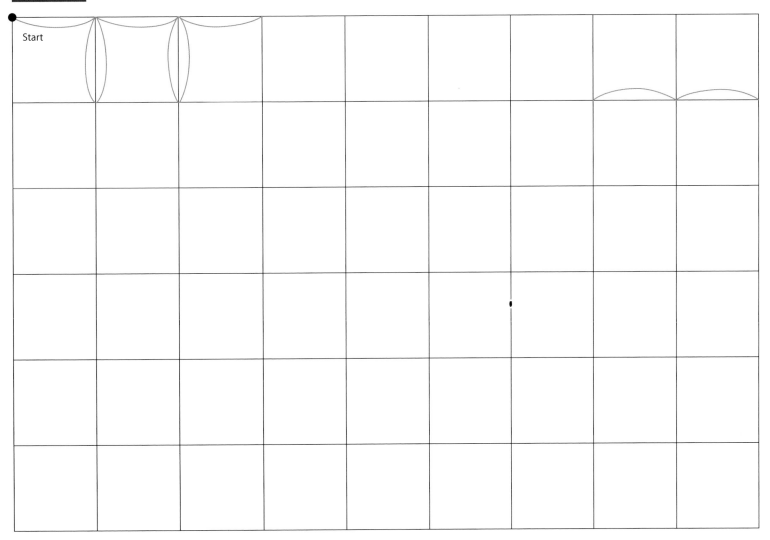

Start

TALK YOURSELF THROUGH THE DESIGN.

First line of design: Over • Down • Up • Over • Down • Up. Repeat to the end of the row, ending in a down curve.

Second line of design: Over • Over. Repeat back to the first square in the row.

Continue the first and second lines of the design to fill the entire practice grid.

When the grid is filled, the last line of the design (or exit path) is Up • Up • Up, all the way back to the starting point.

BORDER GRID LAYOUT 1

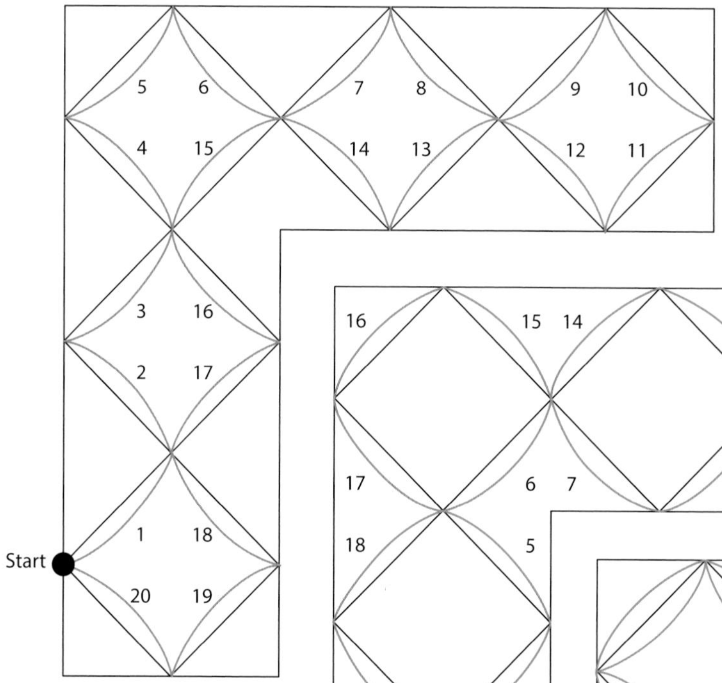

Stitch inside the grid.

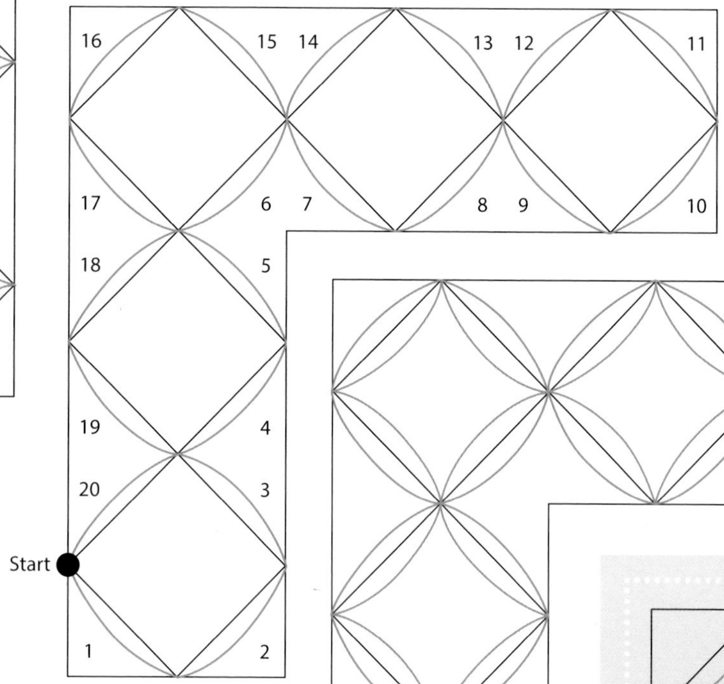

5	6	7	8	9	10
4	15	14	13	12	11

3	16
2	17

1	18
20	19

Start ●

Stitch outside the grid. This pass may feel as if you are moving counterclockwise, but look closely. Within each area, movement is actually clockwise. Look at 5, 6, and 7; do you see how the design moves clockwise?

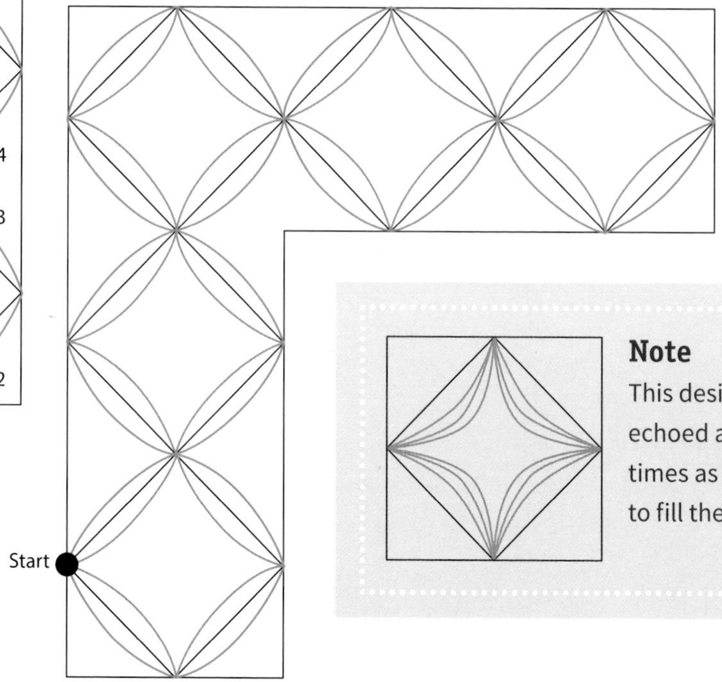

16		15	14		13	12		11
17		6	7		8	9		10
18		5						

19	4
20	3
1	2

Start ●

Stitch both inside and outside the grid.

Start ●

Note

This design can be echoed as many times as needed to fill the space.

BORDER GRID LAYOUT 2

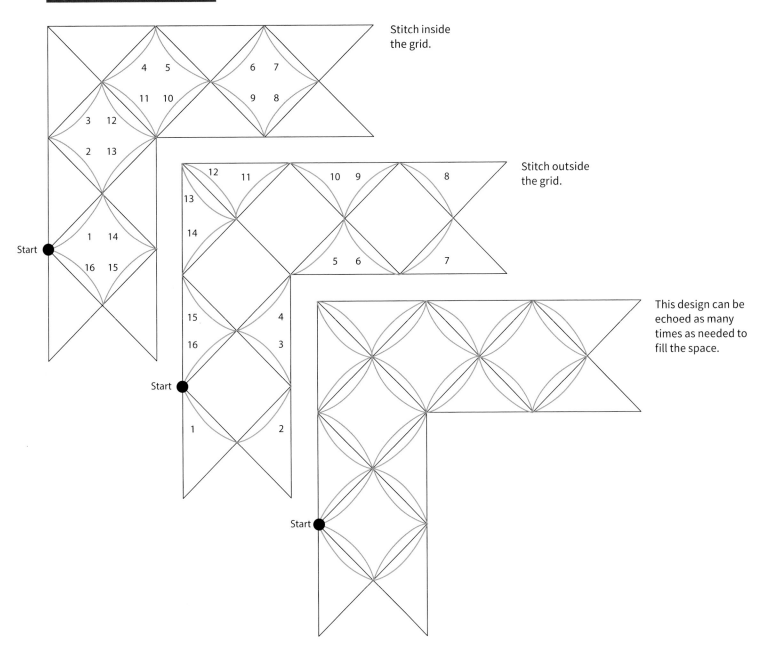

Stitch inside the grid.

Stitch outside the grid.

This design can be echoed as many times as needed to fill the space.

FOUR-PATCH LAYOUT

Follow the numbered sequence. Think of lines 29–32 as your exit path.

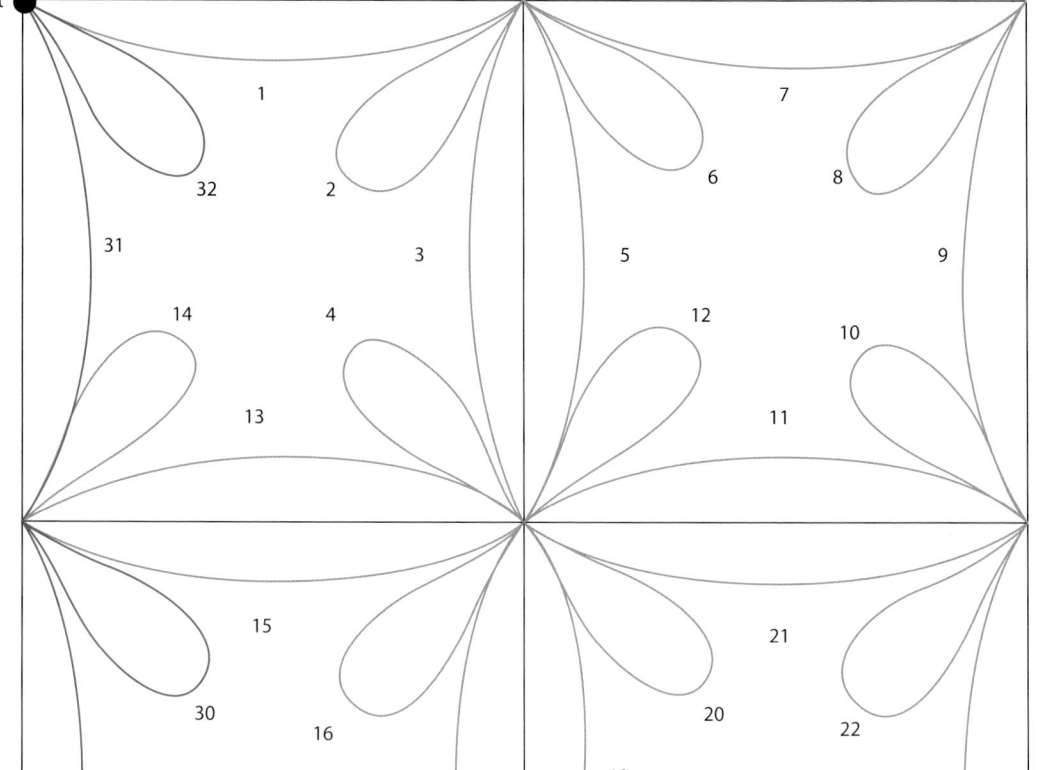

Curve • Petal • Curve • Petal

Start

TALK YOURSELF THROUGH THE DESIGN.

First line of design: Over • Petal • Down • Petal • Up • Petal. Repeat to the end of the row, ending with a petal at the lower right corner.

Second line of design: Over • Petal • Over • Petal. Repeat back to the first square in the row.

Continue the first and second lines of the design to fill the entire practice grid.

When the grid is filled, the last line of the design (or exit path) is Up • Petal • Up • Petal, all the way back to the starting point.

BORDER GRID LAYOUT 1

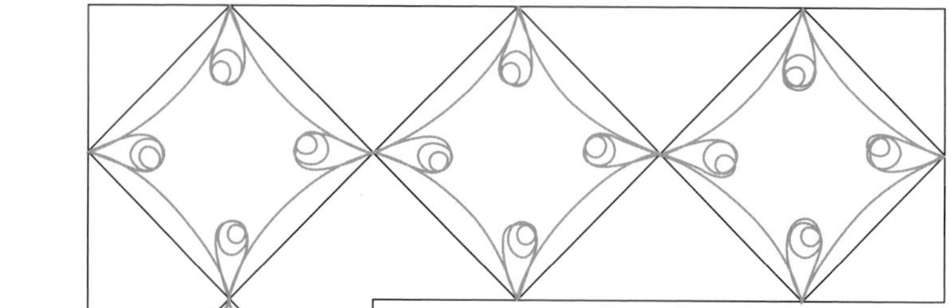

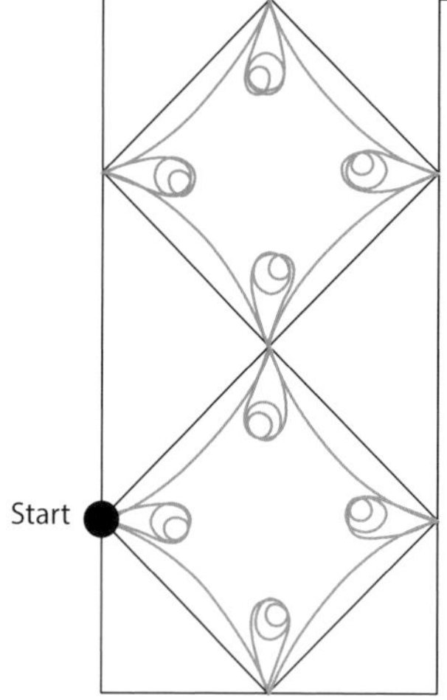

Stitch inside the grid. Try a petal with 1 or 2 circles.

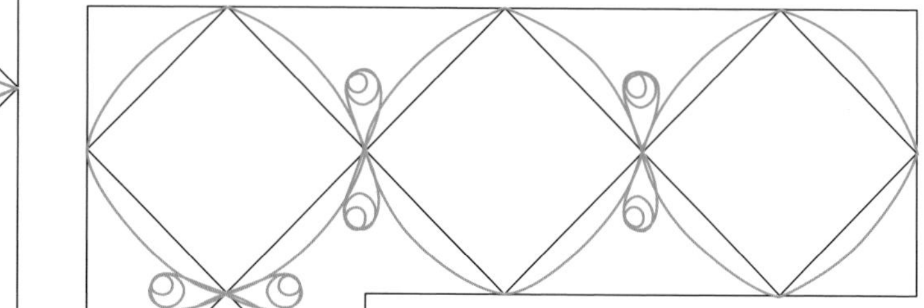

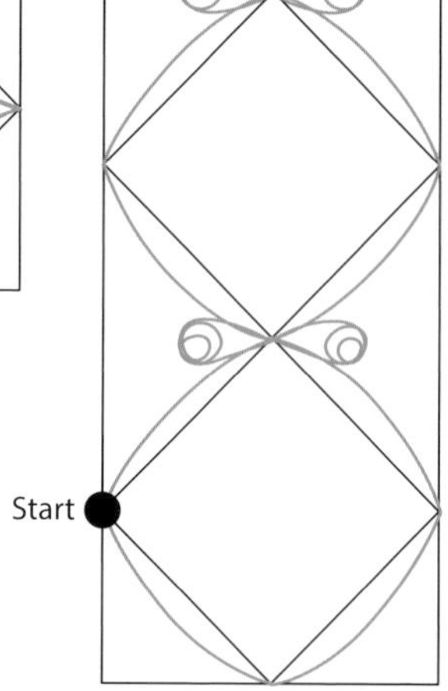

Stitch outside the grid.

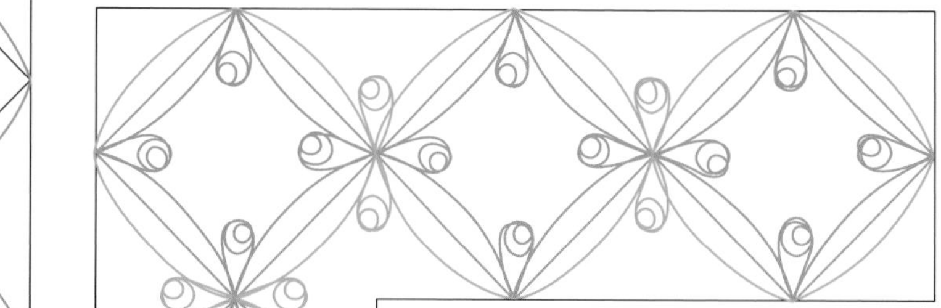

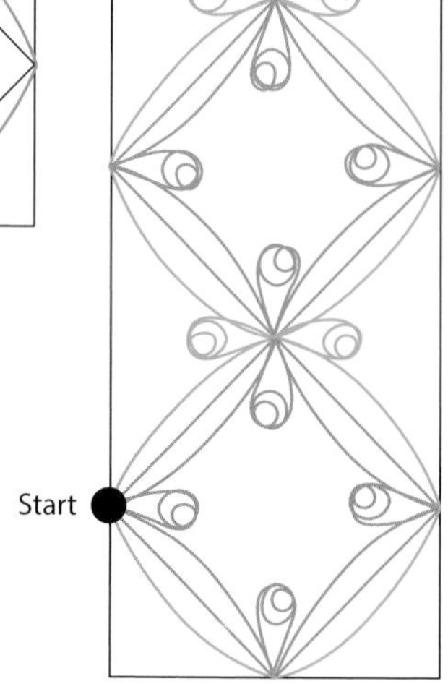

If you want added filler, stitch the straight grid lines first. Then stitch both inside and outside the grid.

Start

Start

Start

DOUBLE-LOOP PETAL

Step 1   Step 2   Step 3   Step 4

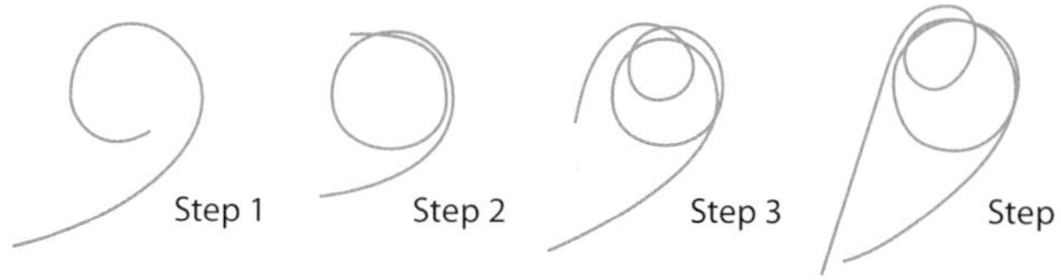

BORDER GRID LAYOUT 2

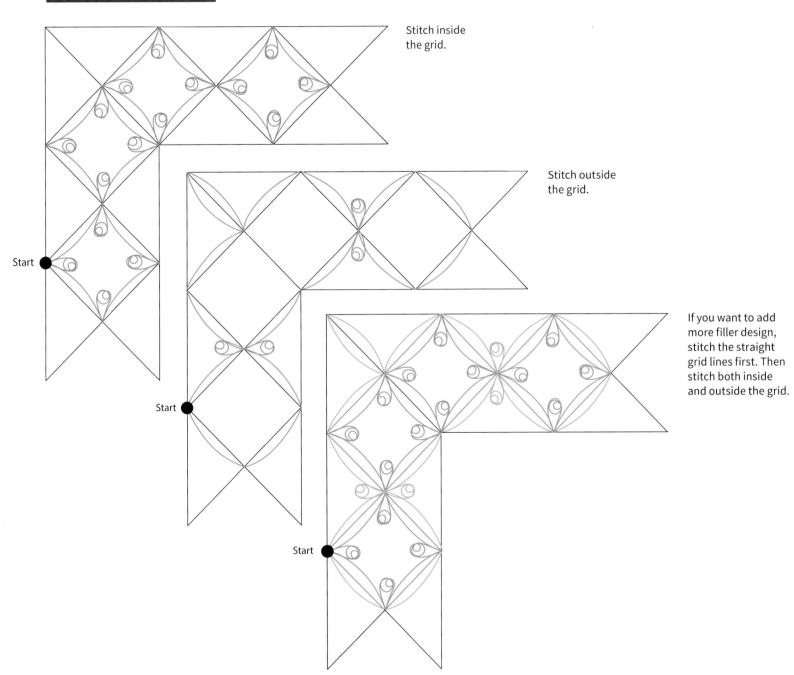

Stitch inside
the grid.

Stitch outside
the grid.

If you want to add
more filler design,
stitch the straight
grid lines first. Then
stitch both inside
and outside the grid.

Start

Start

Start

FOUR-PATCH LAYOUT

Follow the numbered sequence. Which lines make up your exit path?

Start

32	1	2	6	7	8
31		3	5		9
14	13	4	12	11	10
30	15	16	20	21	22
29		17	19		23
28	27	18	26	25	24

Curve • Spike • Spike • Curve • Spike • Spike

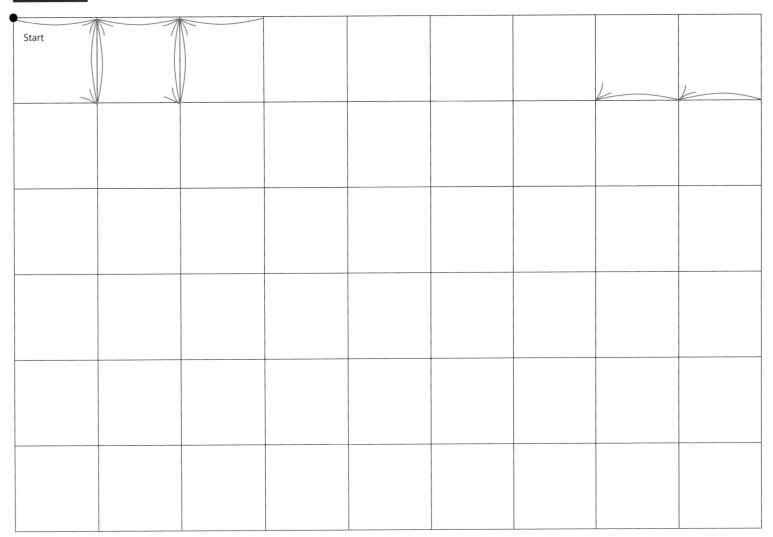

Start

TALK YOURSELF THROUGH THE DESIGN.

First line of design: Over • Spike • Spike • Down • Spike • Spike • Up • Spike • Spike. Repeat to the end of the row, ending in a Spike • Spike at the lower right corner.

Second line of design: Over • Spike • Spike • Over • Spike • Spike. Return back to the first square in the row.

Continue the first and second lines of the design to fill the entire practice grid.

When the grid is filled, the last line of the design (or exit path) is Up • Spike • Spike • Up • Spike • Spike • Up • Spike • Spike, all the way back to the starting point.

SNOWFLAKE

Start

Tip • This is a great design to use for representing snowflakes.

Stitch both for more detail.

Stitch outside the grid.

Stitch inside the grid.

Start

Start

Start

BORDER GRID LAYOUT 1

BORDER GRID LAYOUT 2

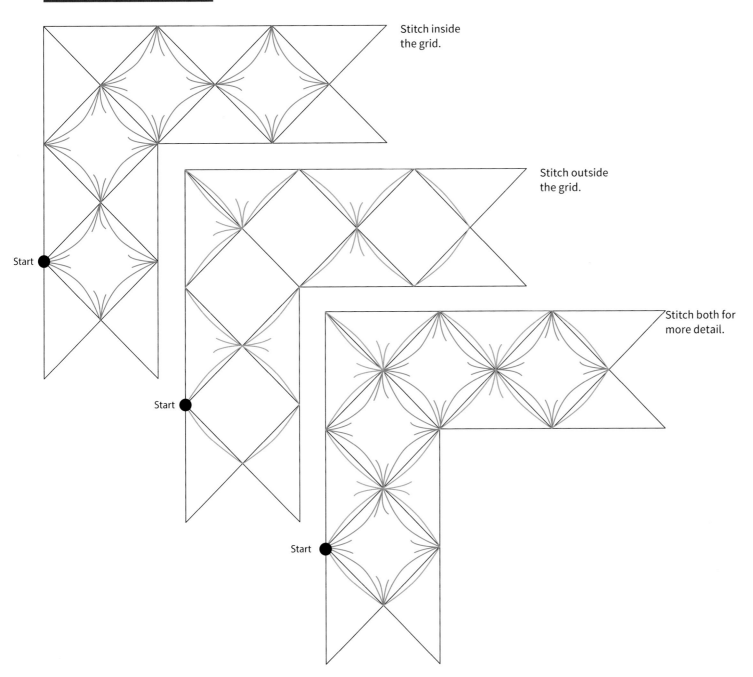

Stitch inside the grid.

Stitch outside the grid.

Stitch both for more detail.

Start

Start

Start

Connecting Curves with Leaves

Curve • Leaf • Curve • Curve • Leaf • Curve • Curve • Leaf • Curve

FOUR-PATCH LAYOUT

Finish the numbered sequence. Add the leaf vein when the leaf shape is completed (see 4, 9, 14, and 19).

Start

PRACTICE

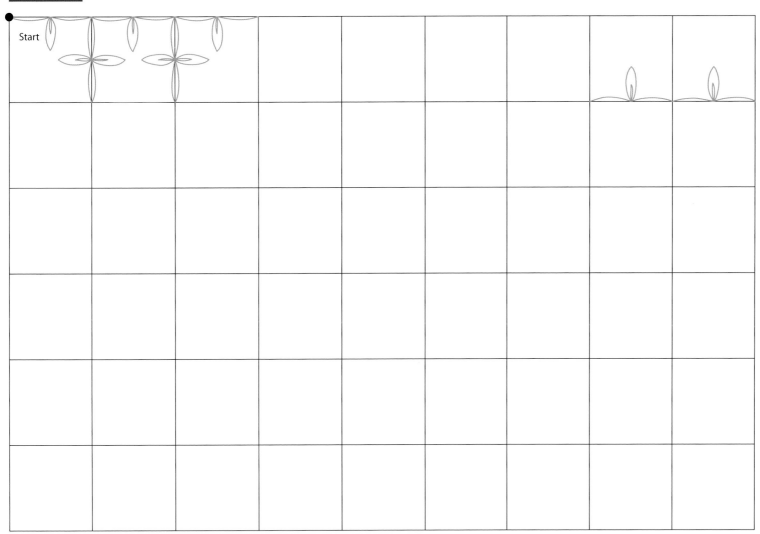

Start

TALK YOURSELF THROUGH THE DESIGN.

First line of design: Over • Leaf • Over • Down • Leaf • Down • Up • Leaf • Up. Repeat to the end of the row, ending in a down curve.

Second line of design: Curve • Leaf • Curve • Curve • Leaf • Curve. Return back to the first square in the row.

Repeat the first and second lines of the design to fill the entire practice grid.

When the grid is filled, the last line of the design (or exit path) is Up • Leaf • Up • Up • Leaf • Up, all the way back to the starting point.

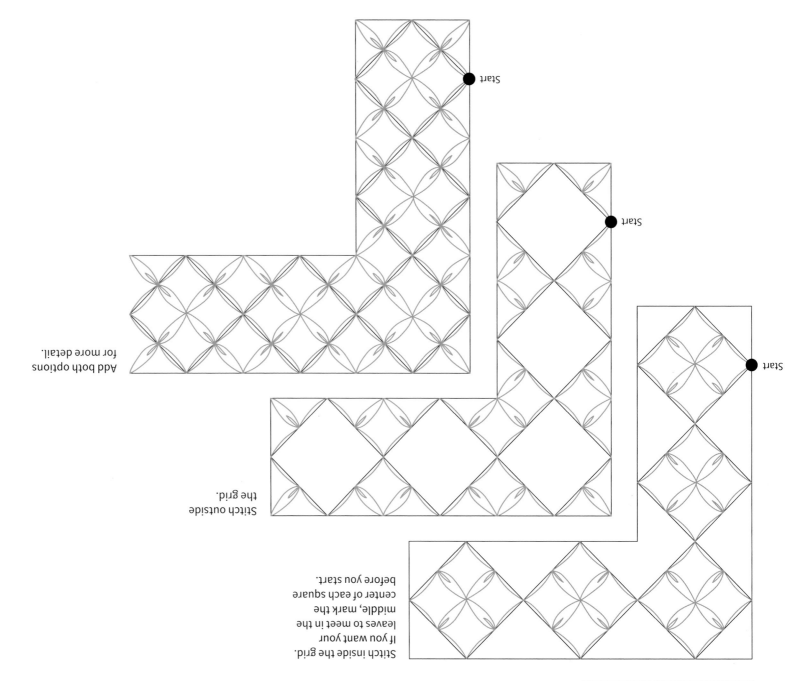

Start

Start

Start

Add both options
for more detail.

Stitch outside
the grid.

Stitch inside the grid.
If you want your
leaves to meet in the
middle, mark the
center of each square
before you start.

BORDER GRID LAYOUT 1

BORDER GRID LAYOUT 2

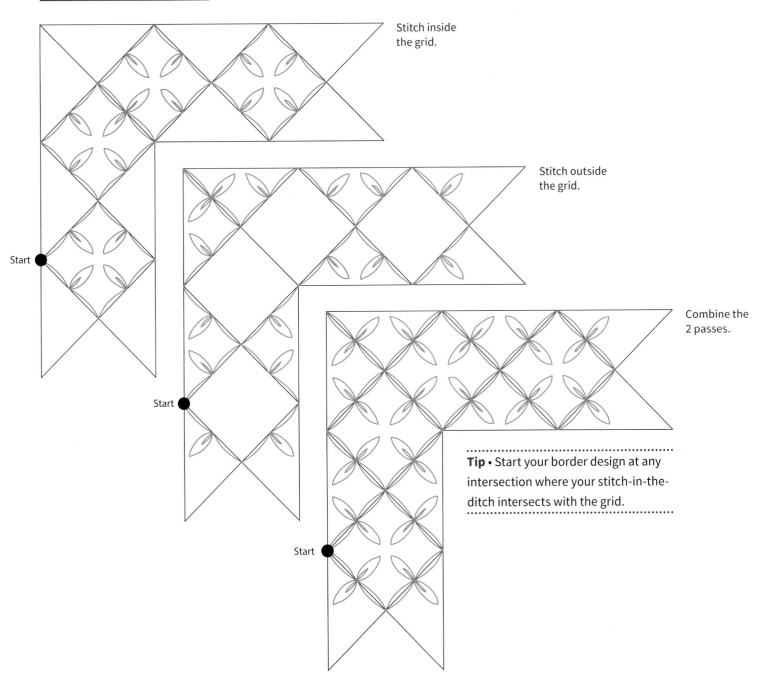

Stitch inside the grid.

Stitch outside the grid.

Combine the 2 passes.

Start

Start

Start

Tip • Start your border design at any intersection where your stitch-in-the-ditch intersects with the grid.

FOUR-PATCH LAYOUT

Follow the numbered sequence. By now the flow through the block should be second nature.

Start

1
7
32   2   6   8
31   3   5   9
14   4   12   10
13   11
15   21
30   20   22
16
29   19   23
17
28   18   26   24
27   25

Curve • Curl • Curve • Curl

PRACTICE

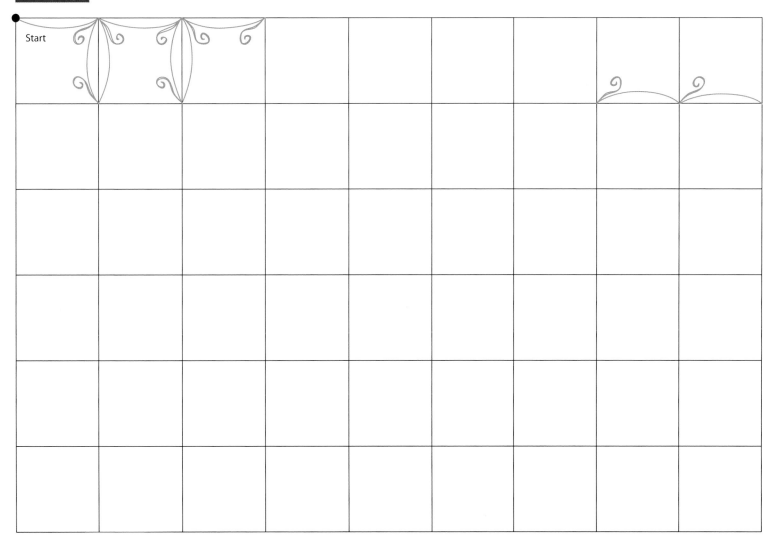

Start

TALK YOURSELF THROUGH THE DESIGN.

First line of design: Over • Curl • Down • Curl • Up • Curl. Repeat to the end of the row, ending in a Down • Curl.

Second line of design: Over • Curl • Over • Curl. Return to the first square in the row.

Repeat the first and second lines of the design to fill the entire practice grid.

When the grid is filled, the last line of the design (or exit path) is Up • Curl • Up • Curl • Up • Curl, all the way back to the starting point.

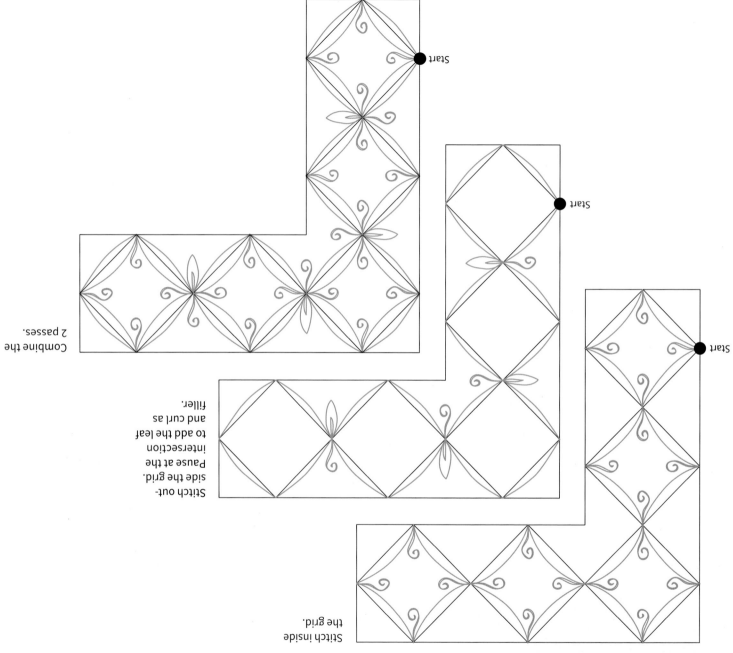

Start

Start

Start

Combine the 2 passes.

Stitch out-
side the grid.
Pause at the
intersection
to add the leaf
and curl as
filler.

Stitch inside
the grid.

BORDER GRID LAYOUT 1

BORDER GRID LAYOUT 2

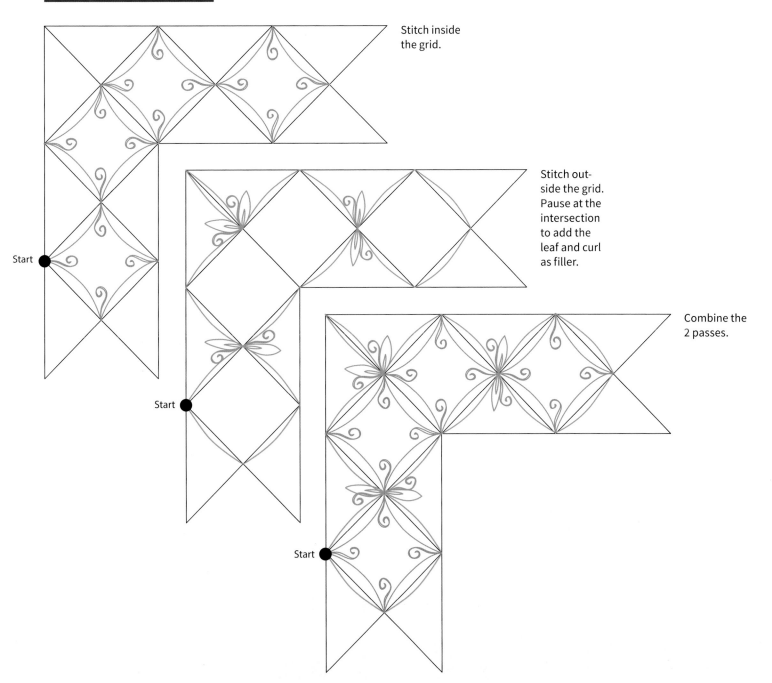

Stitch inside the grid.

Start

Stitch outside the grid. Pause at the intersection to add the leaf and curl as filler.

Start

Combine the 2 passes.

Start

FOUR-PATCH LAYOUT

Follow the numbered sequence.

Over the hill and down

Start

TALK YOURSELF THROUGH THE DESIGN.

First line of design: Over • Down • Up • Over • Down • Up. Repeat to the end of the row, ending in a down curve.

Second line of design: Over • Over. Return to the first square in the row.

Repeat the first and second lines of the design to fill the entire practice grid.

When the grid is filled, the last line of the design (or exit path) is Up • Up • Up, all the way back to the starting point.

Note

Practice drawing the wave: over the hill and back down. It's okay that the hills and valleys touch as the waves move around the sides of the square.

BORDER GRID LAYOUT 1

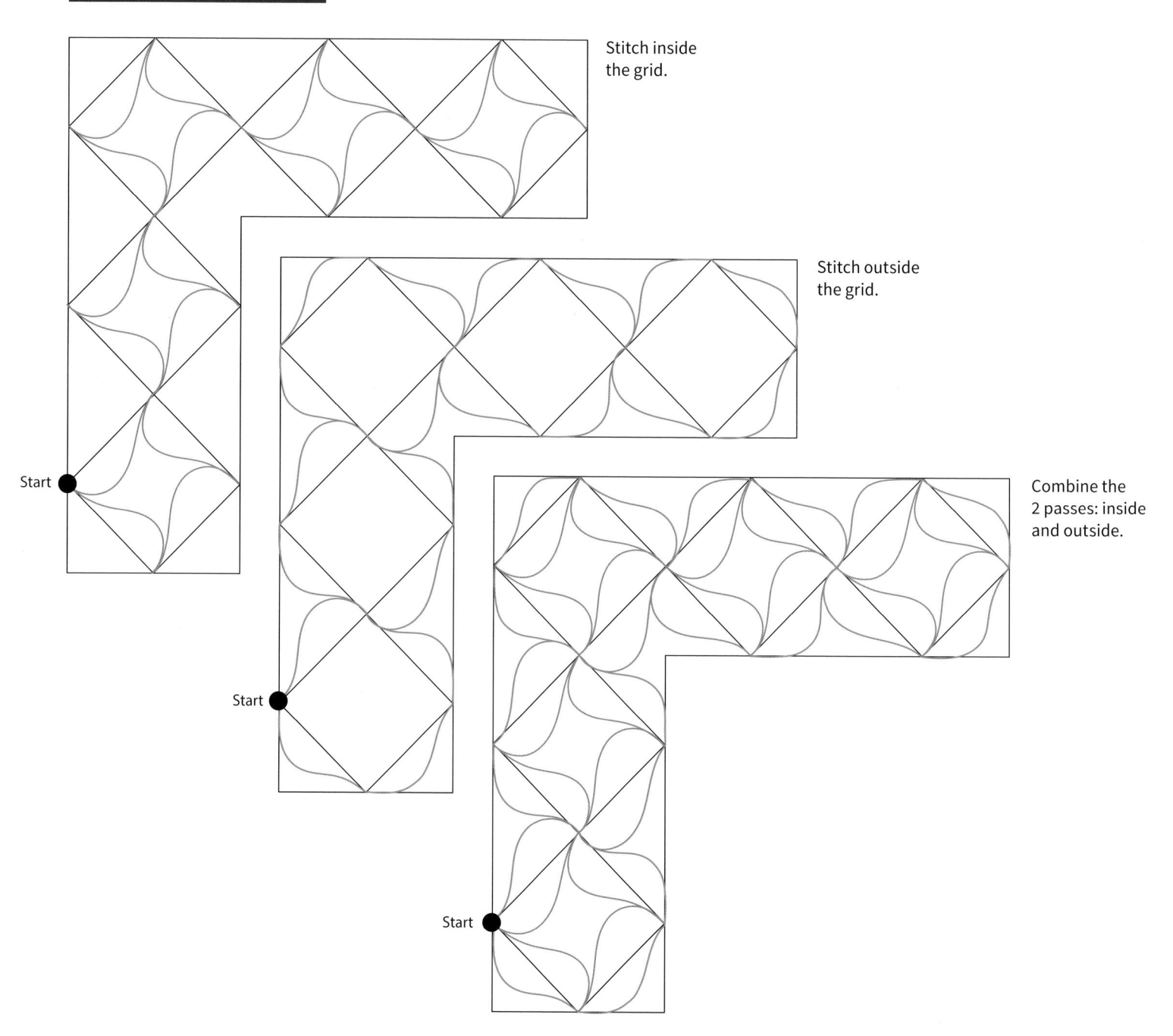

Stitch inside the grid.

Stitch outside the grid.

Combine the 2 passes: inside and outside.

Start

Start

Start

BORDER GRID LAYOUT 2

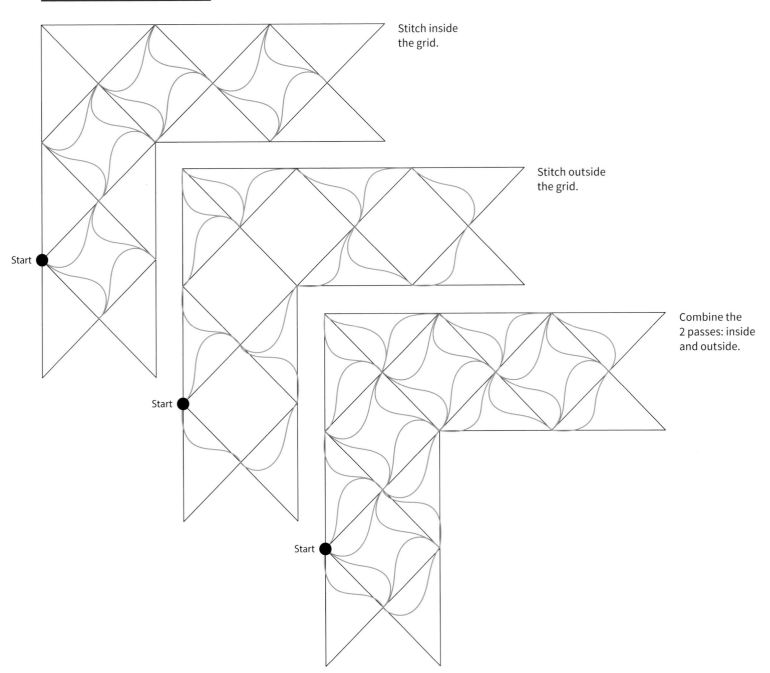

Stitch inside
the grid.

Stitch outside
the grid.

Combine the
2 passes: inside
and outside.

Start

Start

Start

FOUR-PATCH LAYOUT

Follow the numbered sequence. It should be very familiar by now.

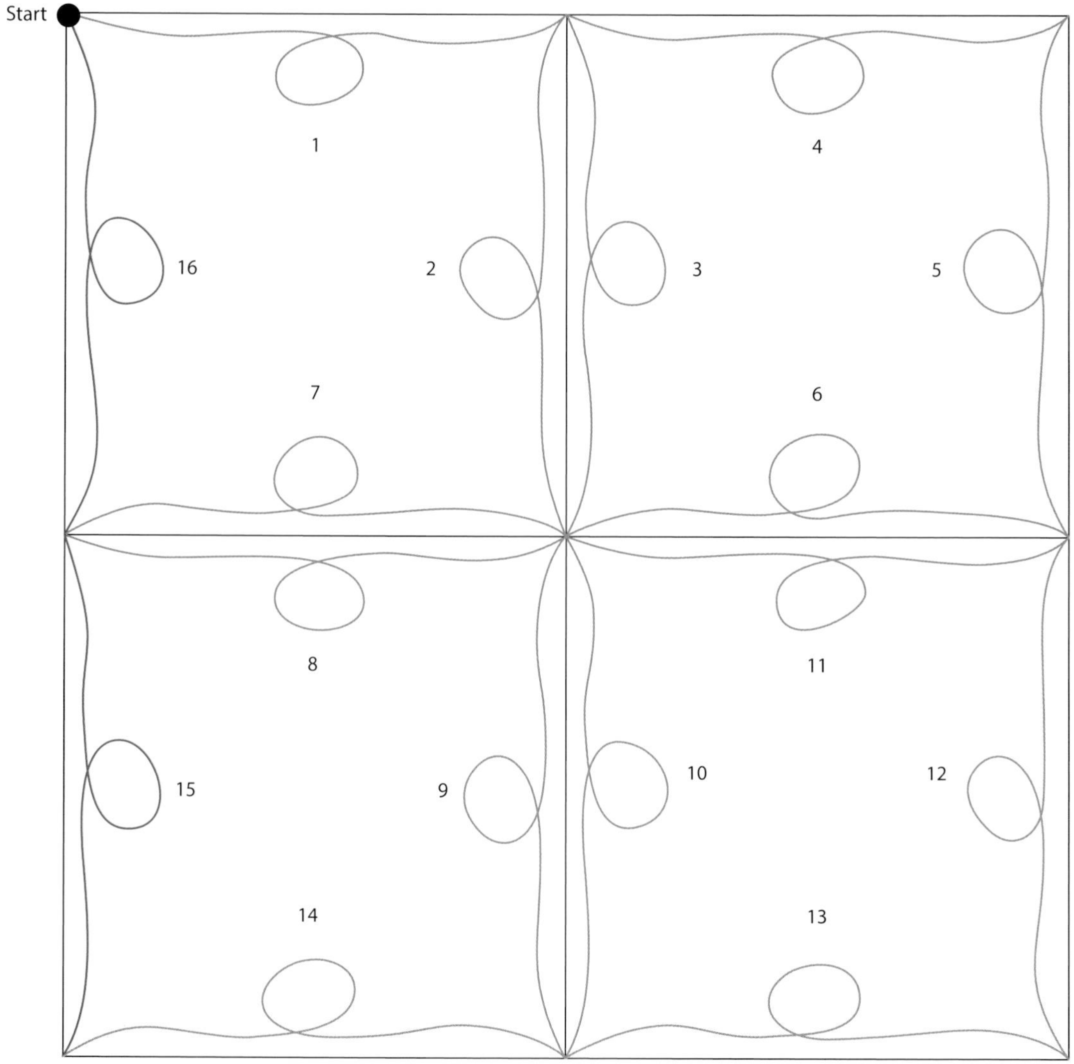

Start

1 4
16 2 3 5
7 6
8 11
15 9 10 12
14 13

Loop • Loop • Loop

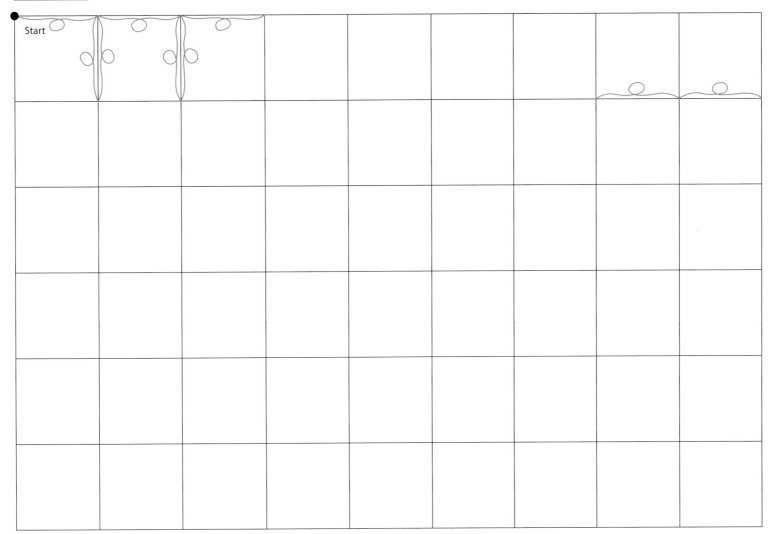

Start

TALK YOURSELF THROUGH THE DESIGN.

First line of design: Over • Down • Up • Over • Down • Up. Repeat to the end of the row, ending in a down loop.

Second line of design: Over • Over. Return to the first square in the row.

Repeat the first and second lines of the design to fill the entire practice grid.

When the grid is filled, the last line of the design (or exit path) is Up • Up • Up, all the way back to the starting point.

BORDER GRID LAYOUT 1

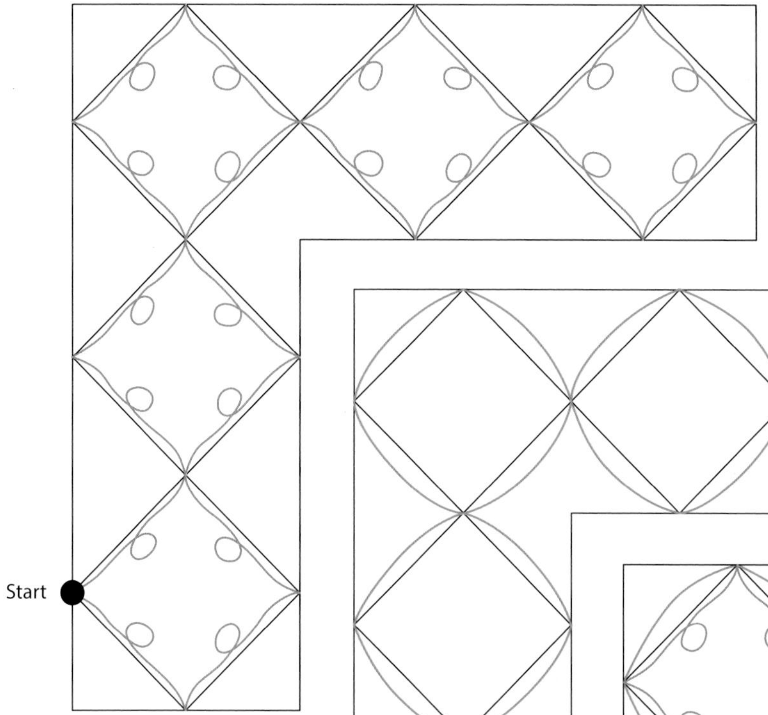

Stitch inside the grid.

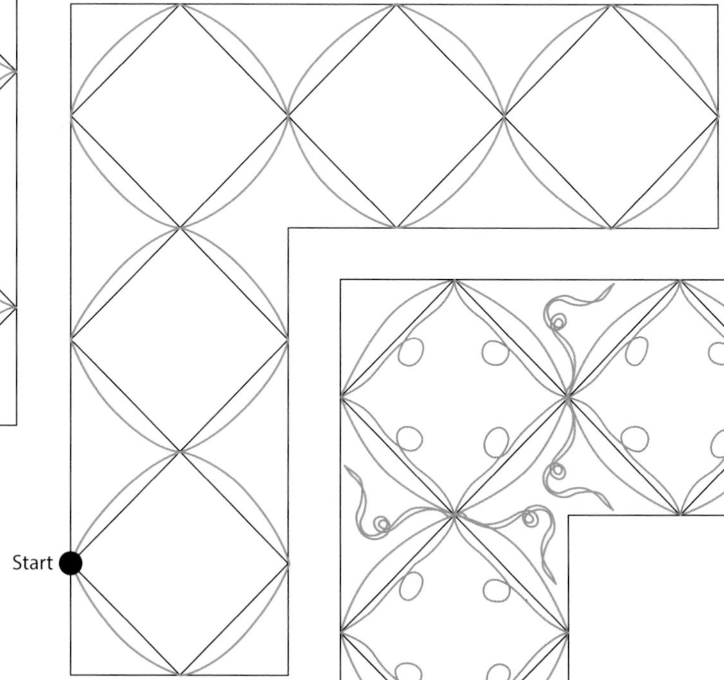

Start

Stitch outside the grid.

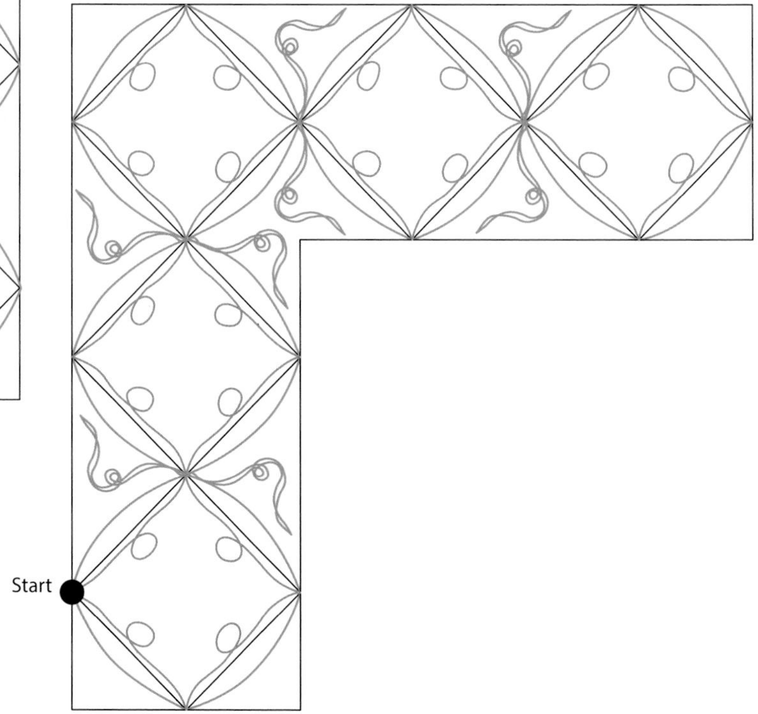

Start

Stitch both passes, plus add filler ribbons on the second pass this time.

Start

BORDER GRID LAYOUT 2

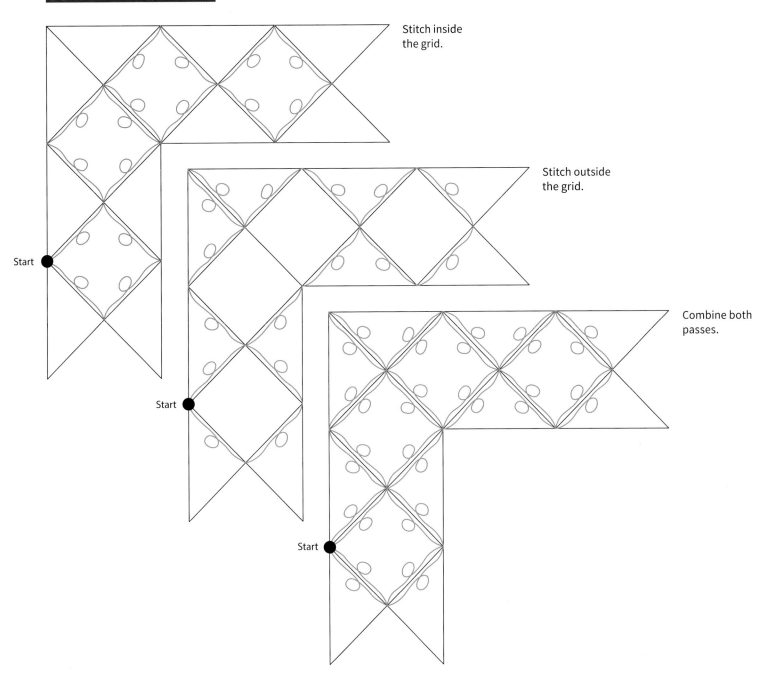

Stitch inside the grid.

Stitch outside the grid.

Combine both passes.

Start

Start

Start

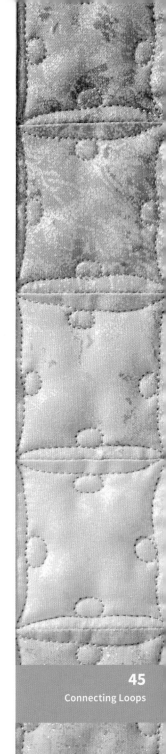

Connecting Curl 1

FOUR-PATCH LAYOUT

Follow the stitching sequence.

Start

1

4

16   2   3   5

7   6

8   11

15   9   10   12

14   13

Curl • Corner • Curl • Corner

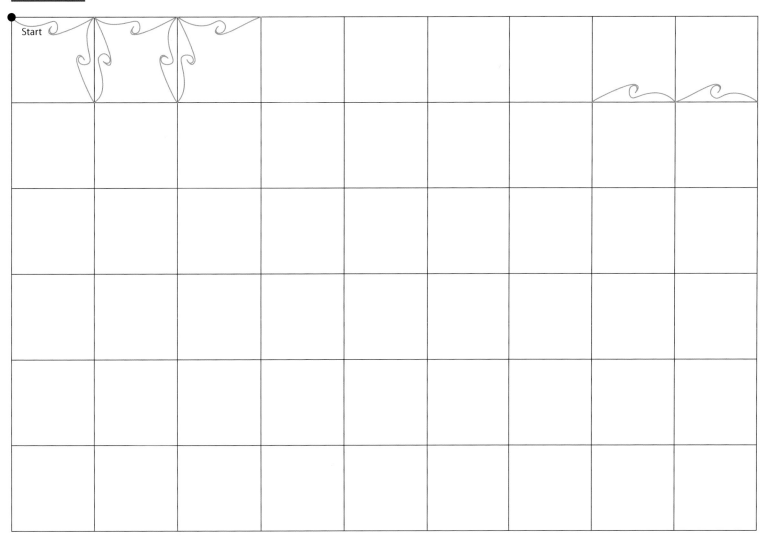

TALK YOURSELF THROUGH THE DESIGN.

First line of design: Over • Down • Up • Over • Down • Up. Repeat to the end of the row, ending in a down curve.

Second line of design: Over • Over. Return to the first square in the row.

Repeat the first and second lines of the design to fill the entire practice grid.

When the grid is filled, the last line of the design (or the exit path) is Up • Up • Up, all the way back to the starting point.

BORDER GRID LAYOUT 1

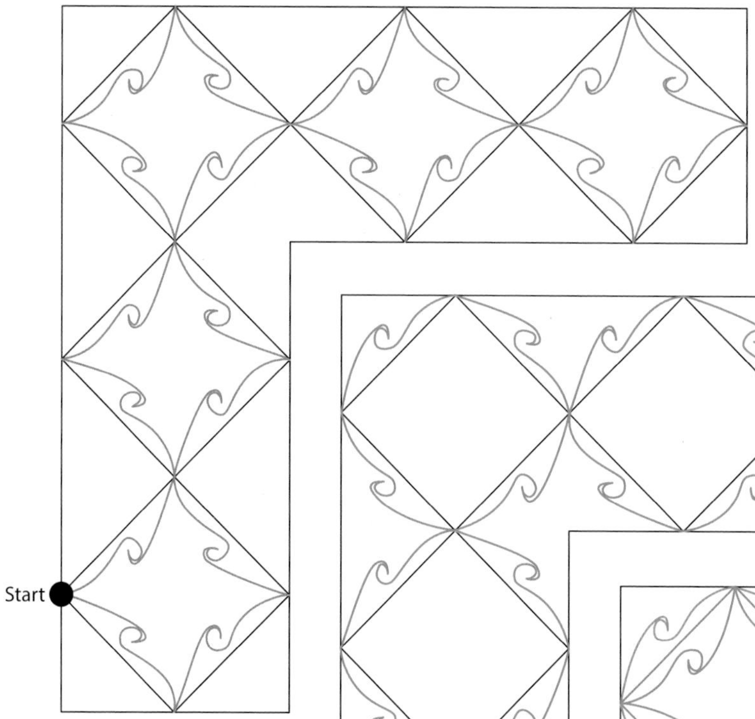

Stitch inside
the grid.

Stitch outside
the grid.

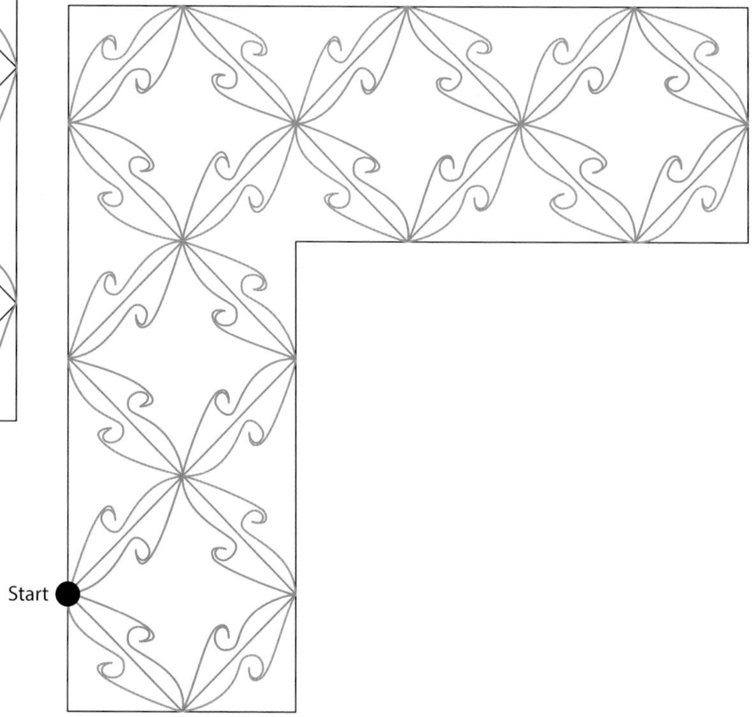

For added filler,
stitch the grid
lines first. Then
stitch inside and
outside the grid.

Start

Start

Start

BORDER GRID LAYOUT 2

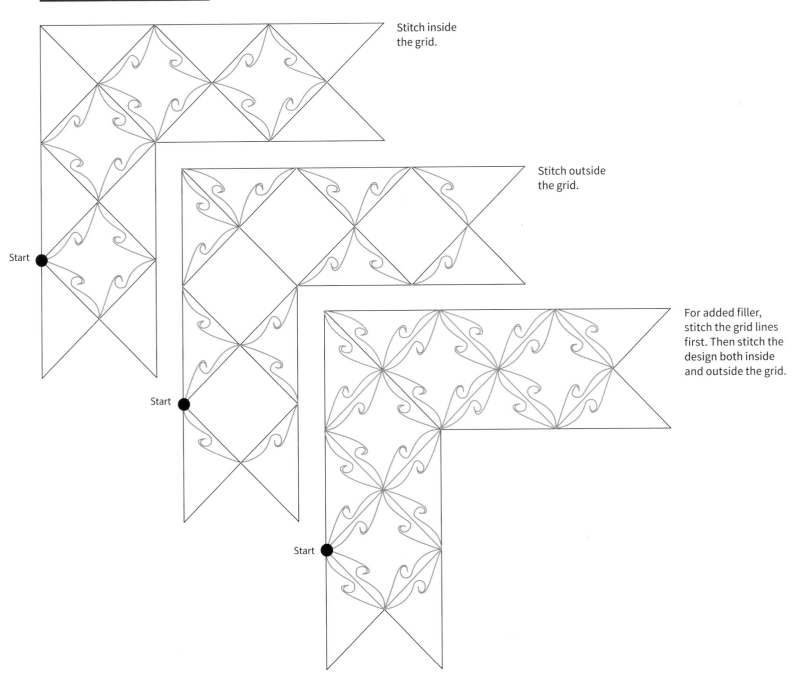

Stitch inside the grid.

Stitch outside the grid.

For added filler, stitch the grid lines first. Then stitch the design both inside and outside the grid.

Start

Start

Start

FOUR-PATCH LAYOUT

Follow the stitching sequence.

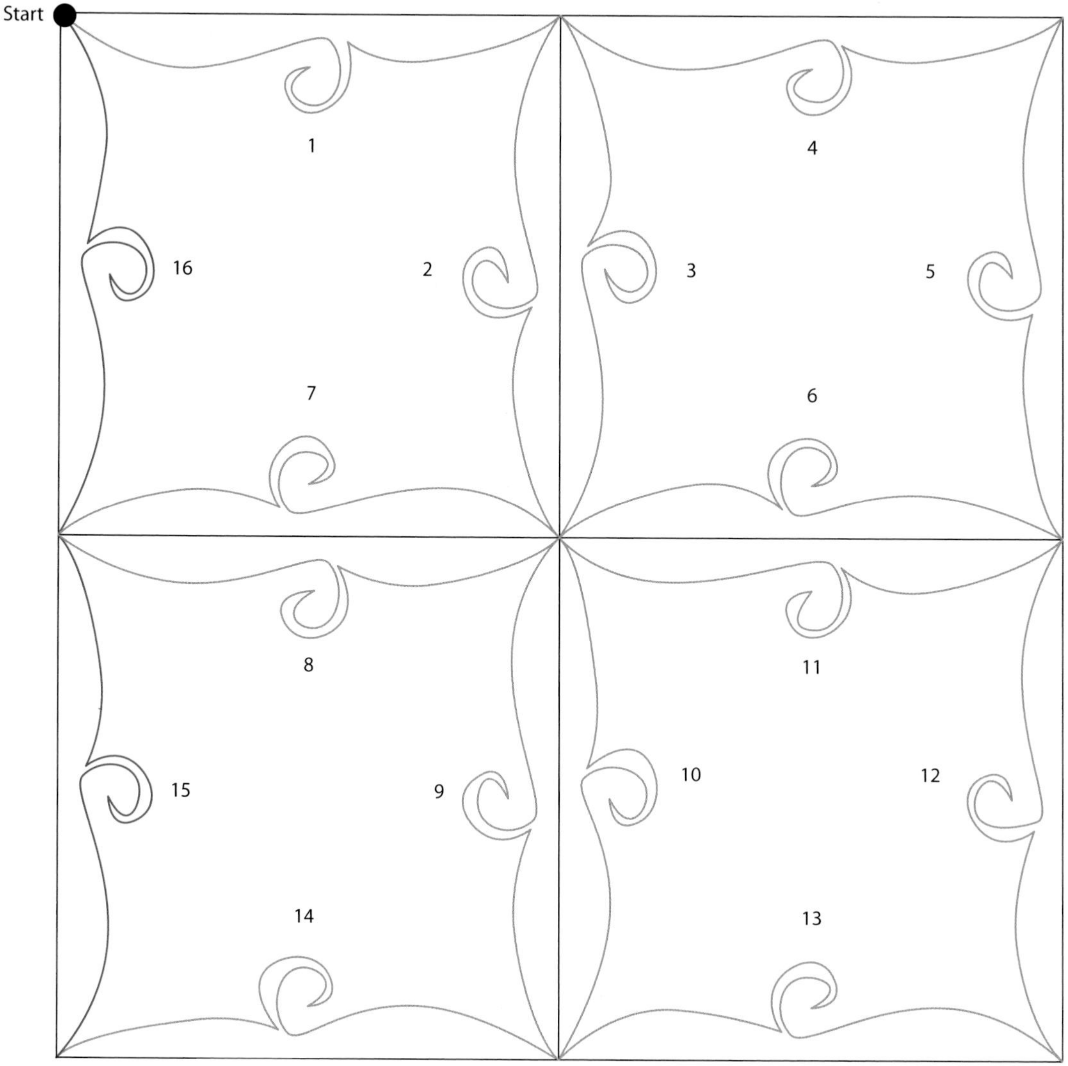

Start

1

16 2

7

4

3 5

6

8

15 9

11

10 12

14

13

Curl • Backtrack • Corner • Curl • Backtrack • Corner

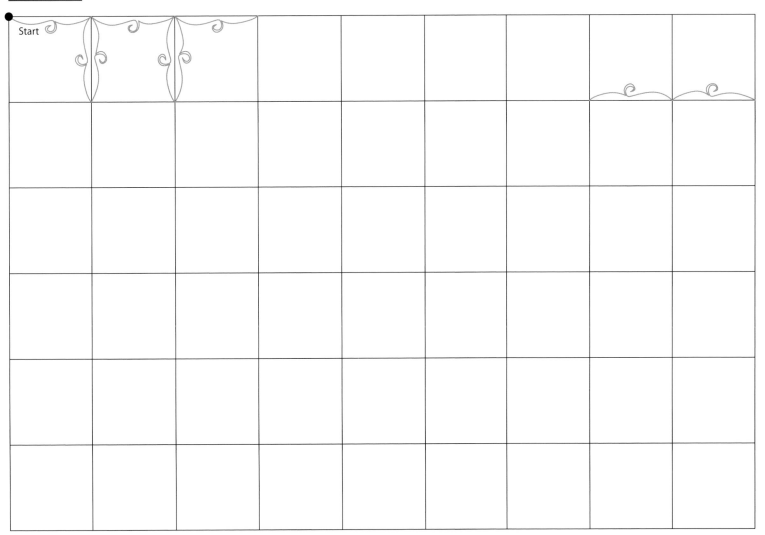

Start

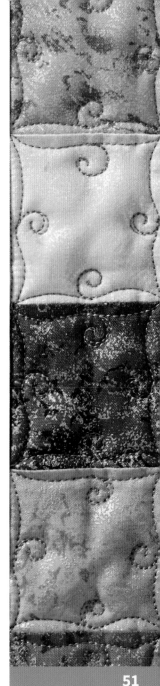

TALK YOURSELF THROUGH THE DESIGN.

First line of design: Over • Down • Up • Over • Down • Up. Repeat to the end of the row, ending in a down curve.

Second line of design: Over • Over. Return to the first square in the row.

Repeat the first and second lines of the design to fill the entire practice grid.

When the grid is filled, the last line of the design (or exit path) is Up • Up • Up, all the way back to the starting point.

Note

Stitch the curl, backtrack along the curl, and then stitch to the intersection.

BORDER GRID LAYOUT 1

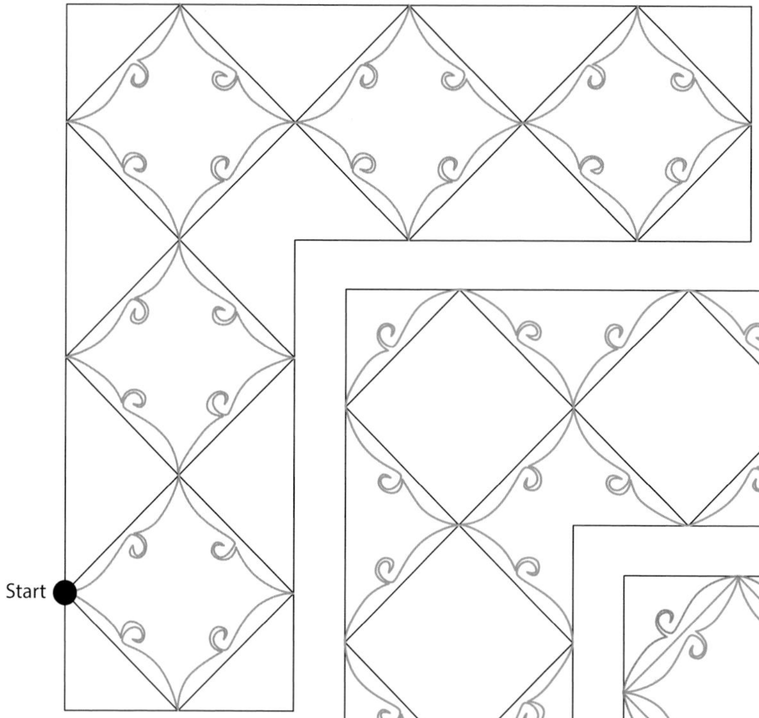

Stitch inside the grid.

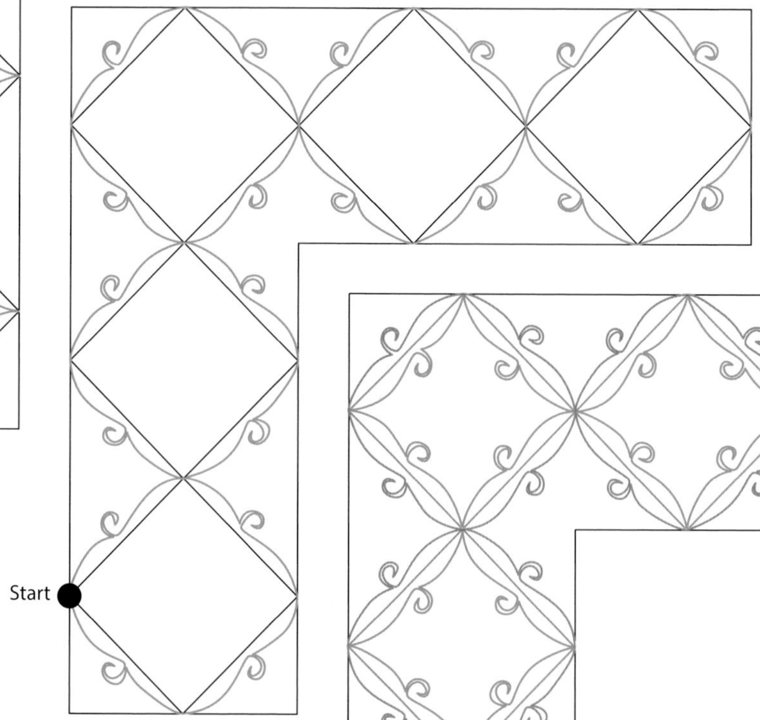

Stitch outside the grid.

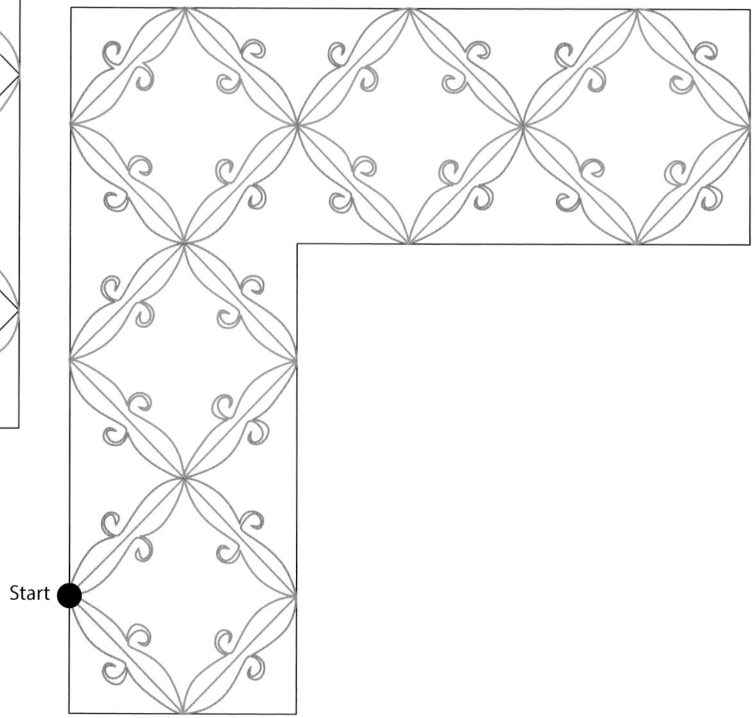

For a fuller design, stitch the straight grid lines first. Then stitch both inside and outside passes.

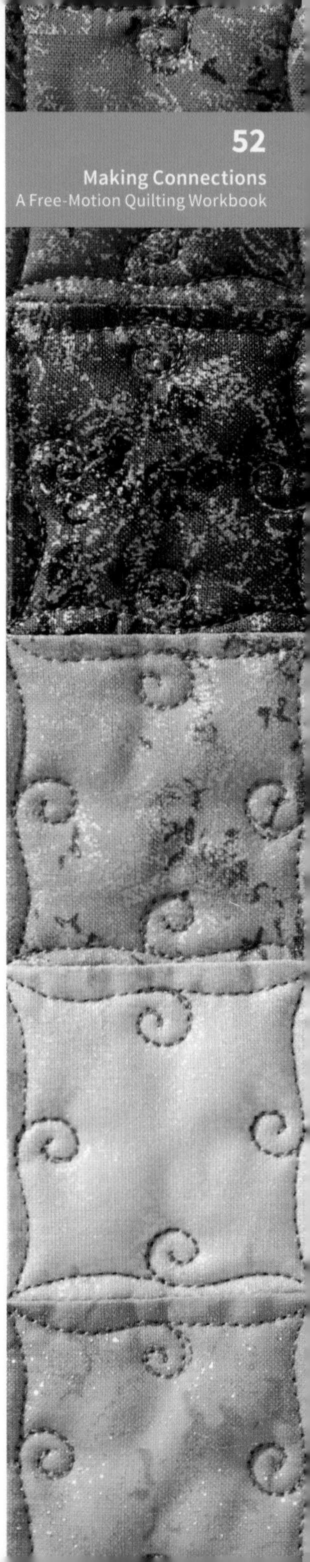

Start

Start

Start

BORDER GRID LAYOUT 2

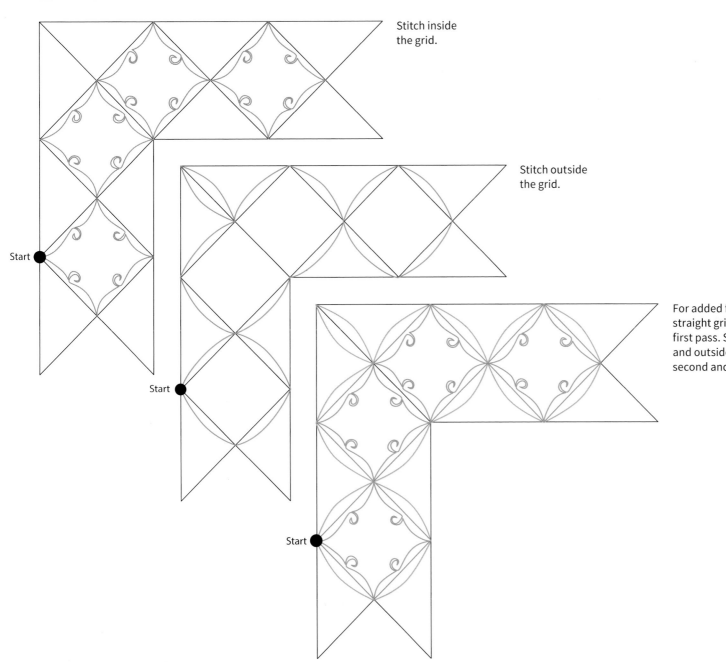

Stitch inside the grid.

Stitch outside the grid.

For added filler, stitch straight grid lines on the first pass. Stitch both inside and outside the grid as second and third passes.

Start

Start

Start

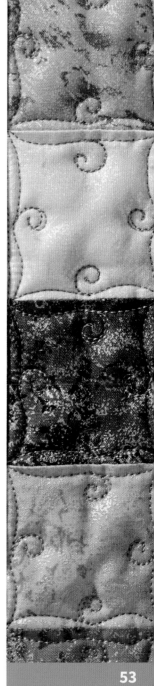

Connecting Double Curls

FOUR-PATCH LAYOUT

Follow the stitching sequence.

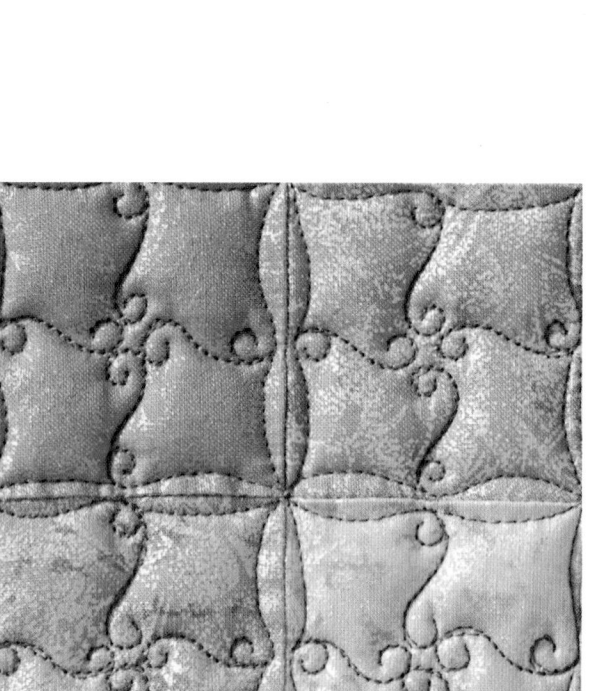

Curl • Backtrack • Curl • Backtrack • Corner

PRACTICE

Start

TALK YOURSELF THROUGH THE DESIGN.

First line of design: Over • Curl • Curl • Over • Down • Curl • Curl • Down • Up • Curl • Curl • Up. Repeat to the end of the row, ending in a down curve.

Second line of design: Over • Curl • Curl • Over. Return to the first square in the row.

Repeat the first and second lines of the design to fill the entire practice grid.

When the grid is filled, the last line of the design (or exit path) is Up • Curl • Curl • Up, all the way back to the starting point.

Note

Stitch the curl, backtrack, add a second curl, backtrack, and complete the line.

BORDER GRID LAYOUT 1

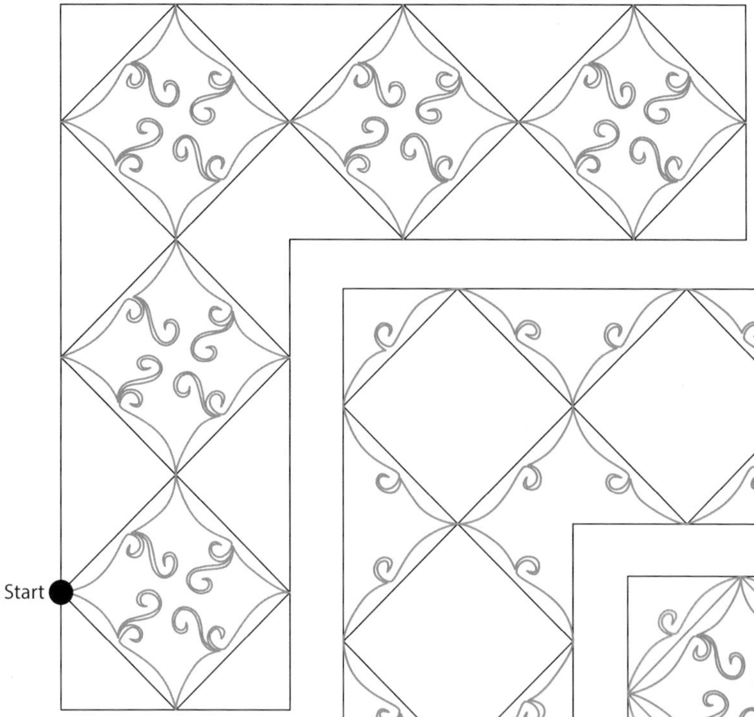

Stitch inside the grid. If you want, mark the center of each square with a dot to have the curls touch.

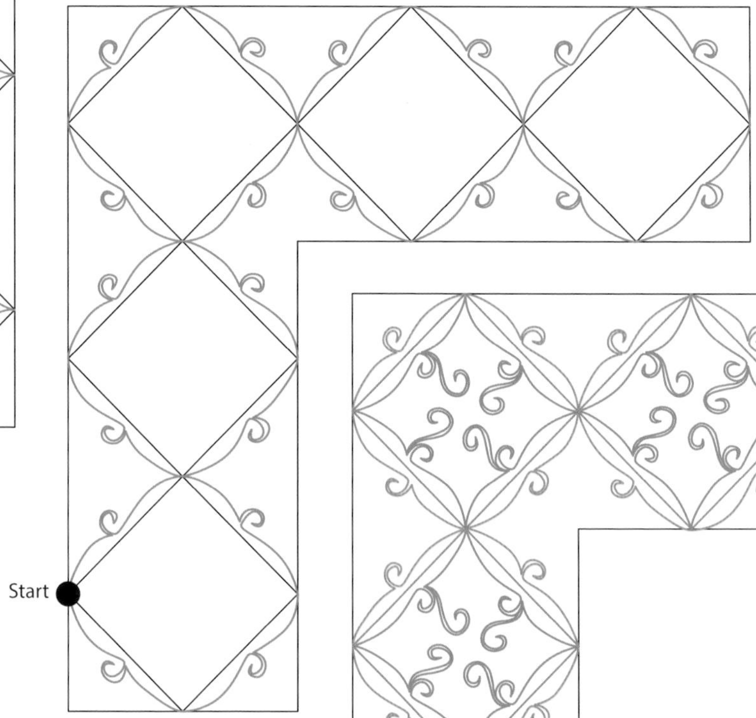

Stitch a single curl outside the grid.

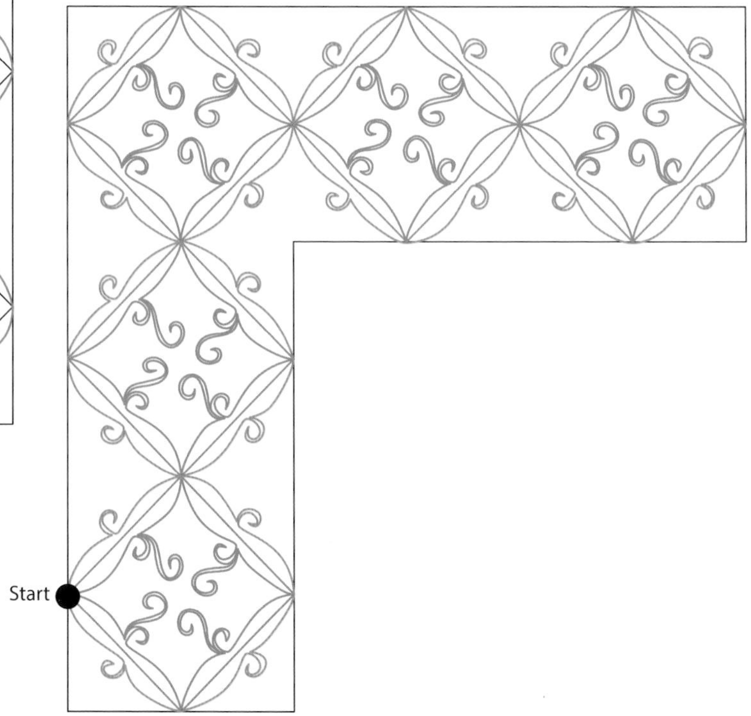

Stitch straight grid lines for a fuller design. Then stitch the remaining 2 passes.

Start

Start

Start

BORDER GRID LAYOUT 2

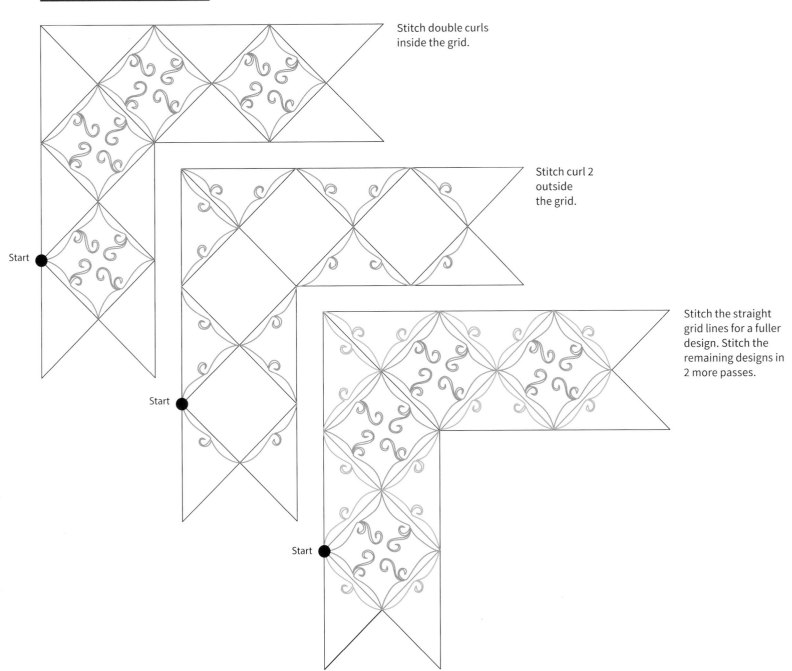

Stitch double curls inside the grid.

Stitch curl 2 outside the grid.

Stitch the straight grid lines for a fuller design. Stitch the remaining designs in 2 more passes.

Start

Start

Start

FOUR-PATCH LAYOUT

Follow the stitching sequence.

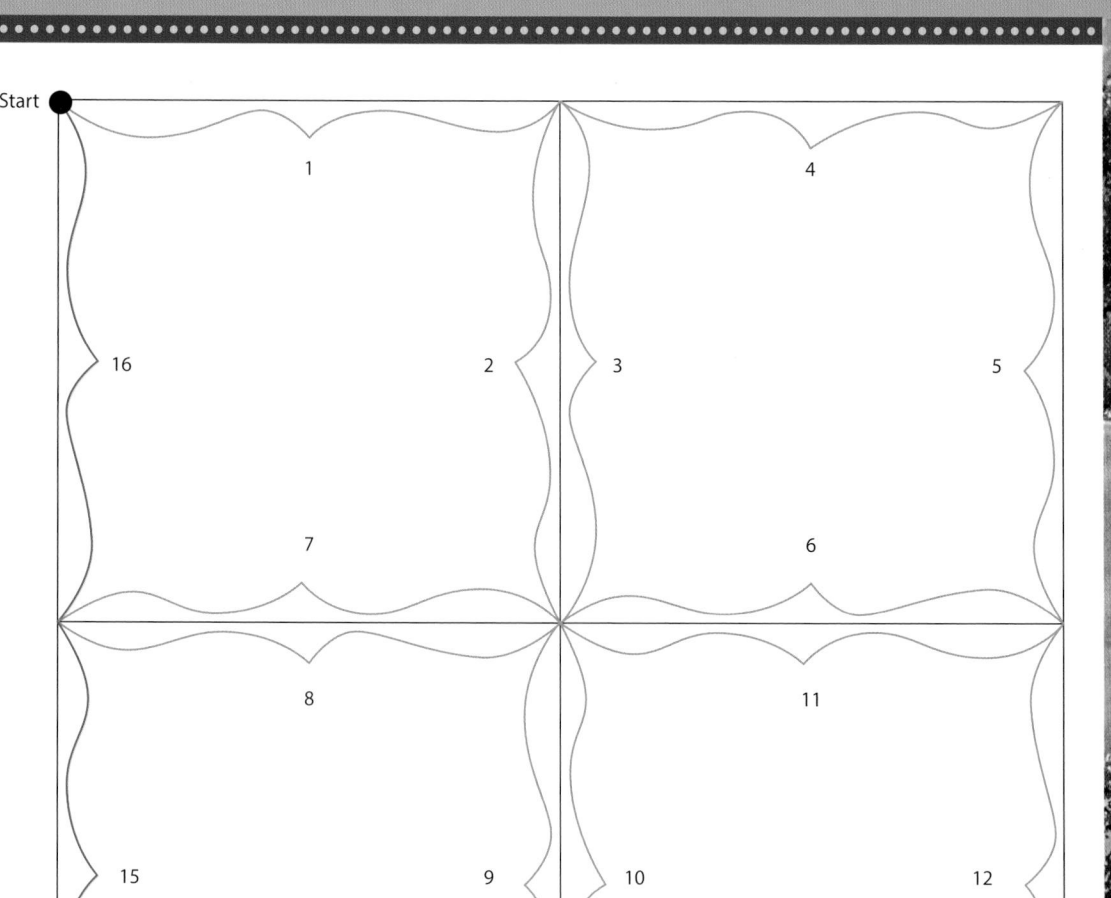

Start

1   4

16   2   3   5

7   6

8   11

15   9   10   12

14   13

Bracket • Bracket • Bracket

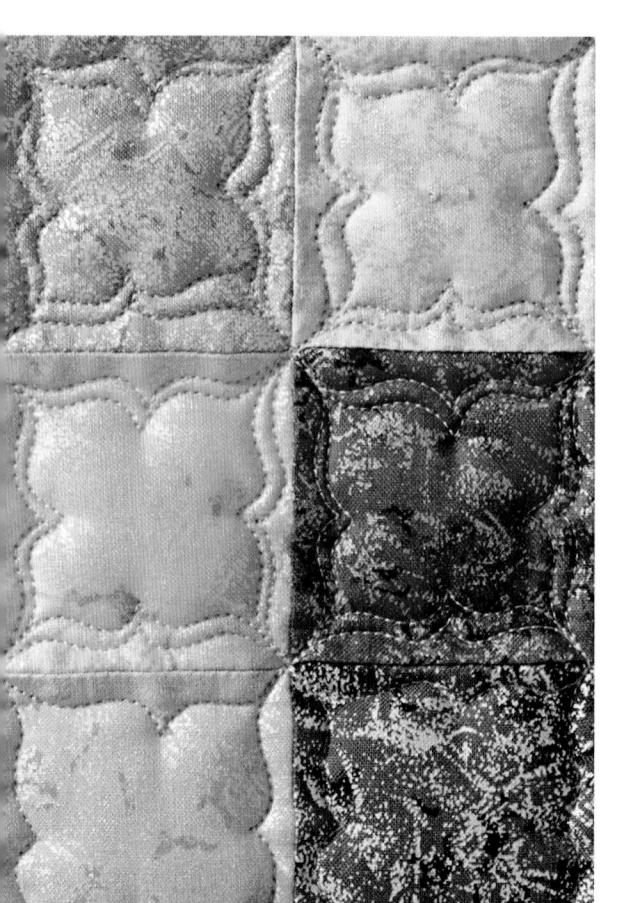

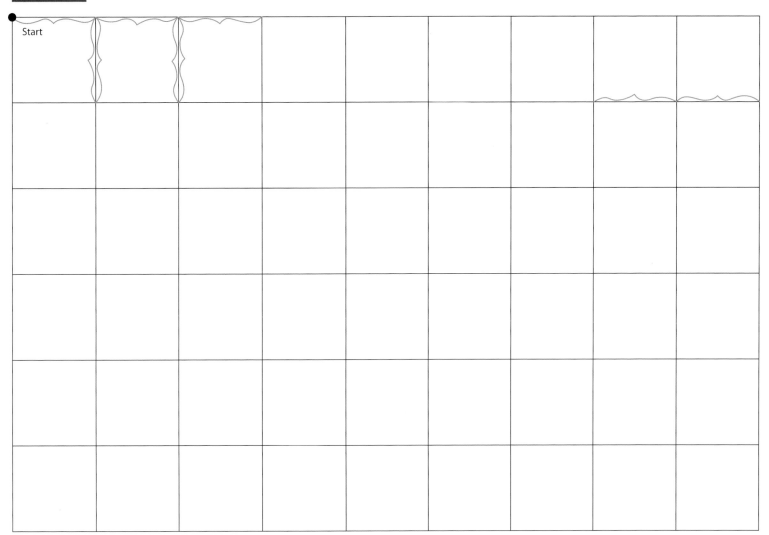

Start

TALK YOURSELF THROUGH THE DESIGN.

First line of design: Over • Down • Up • Over • Down • Up. Repeat to the end of the row, ending in a down curve.

Second line of design: Over • Over. Return to the first square in the row.

Repeat the first and second lines of the design to fill the entire practice grid.

When the grid is filled, the last line of the design (or exit path) is Up • Up • Up, all the way back to the starting point.

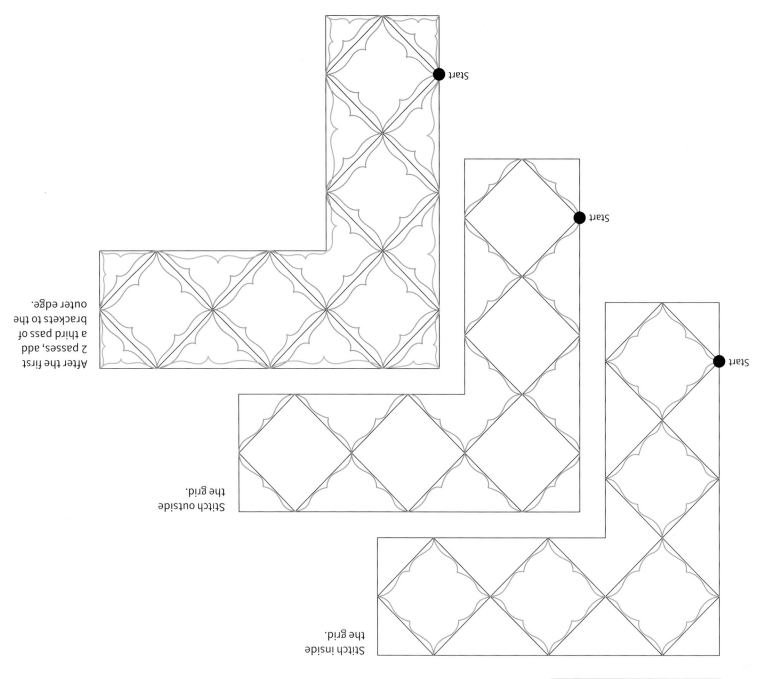

After the first
2 passes, add
a third pass of
brackets to the
outer edge.

Start

Start

Start

Stitch outside
the grid.

Stitch inside
the grid.

BORDER GRID LAYOUT 1

BORDER GRID LAYOUT 2

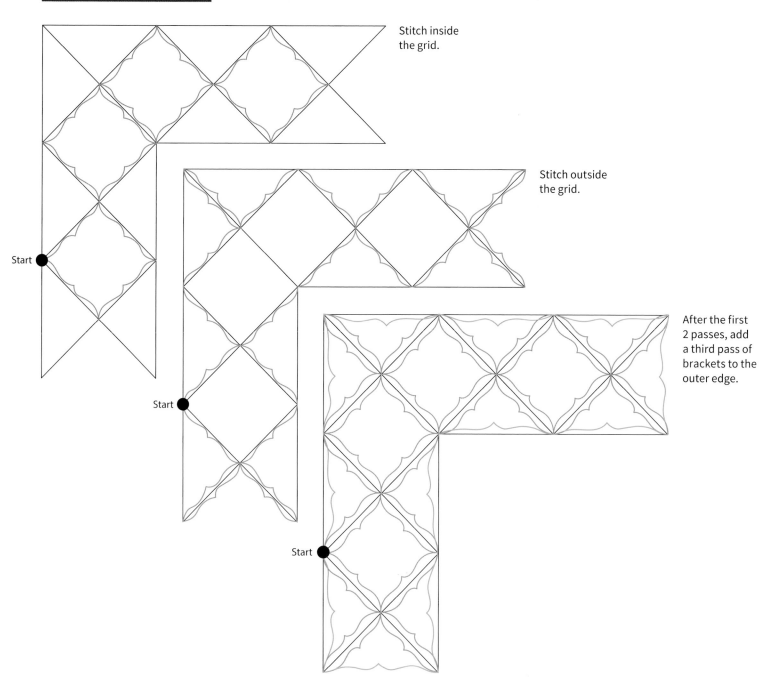

Stitch inside the grid.

Stitch outside the grid.

After the first 2 passes, add a third pass of brackets to the outer edge.

Start

Start

Start

Connecting Brackets with Spikes

FOUR-PATCH LAYOUT

Follow the stitching sequence.

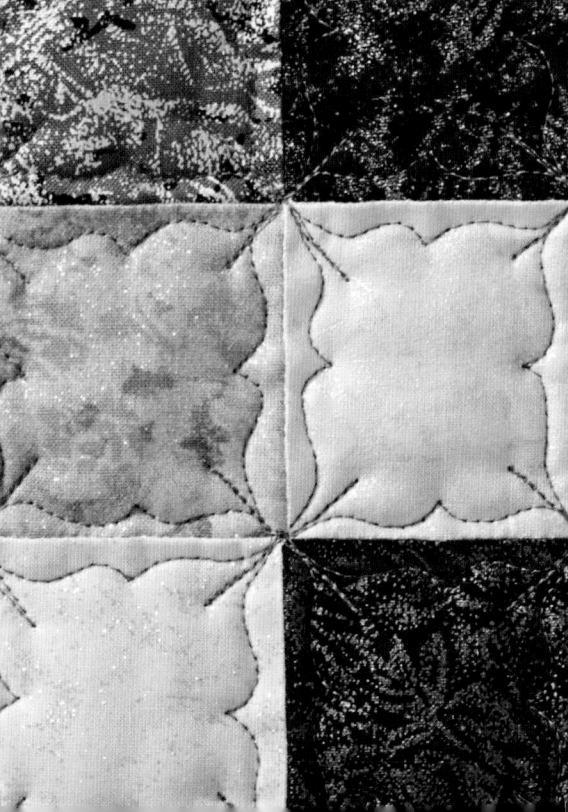

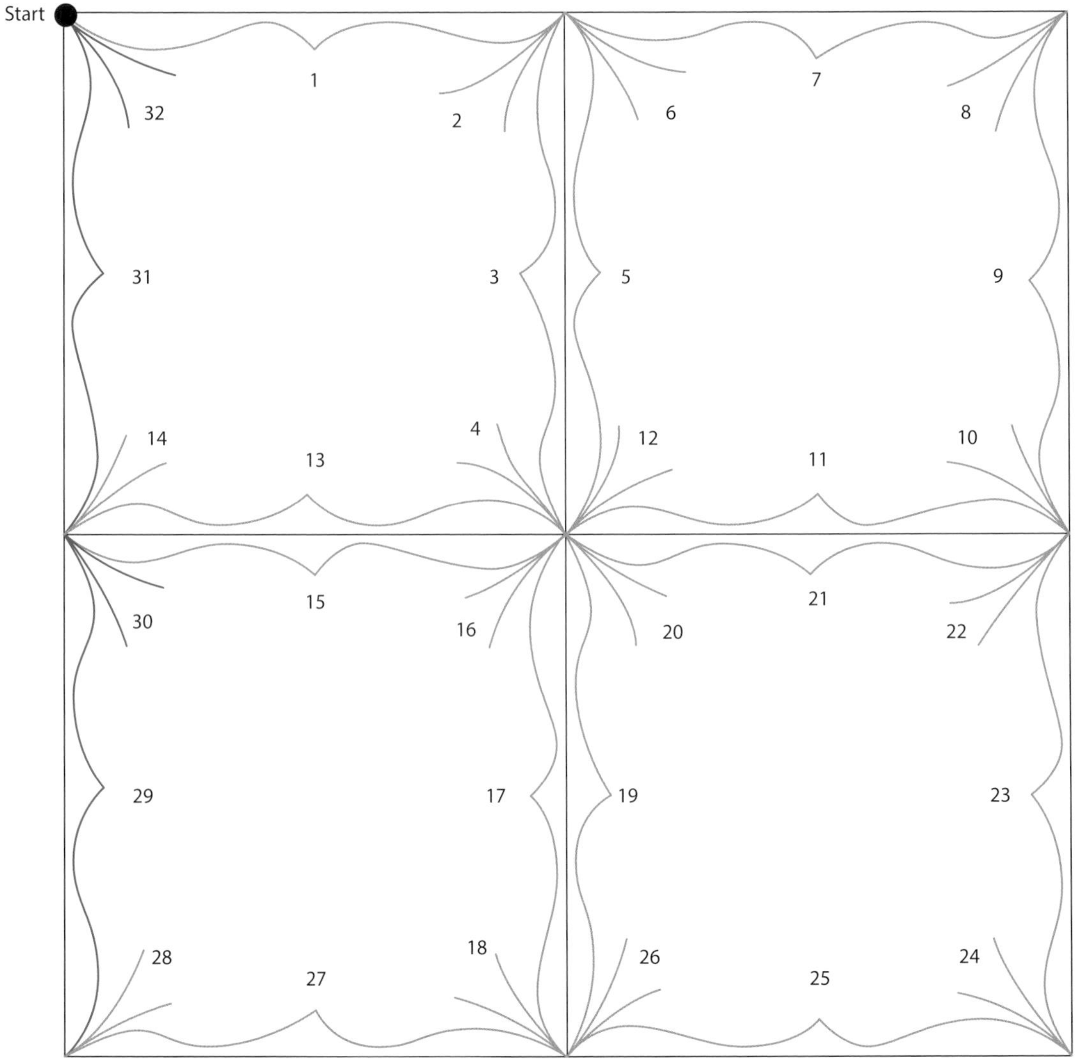
Start
1
32
2
7
6
8
31
3
5
9
14
13
4
12
11
10
15
30
16
21
20
22
29
17
19
23
28
27
18
26
25
24

Bracket • Spike • Spike • Bracket • Spike • Spike

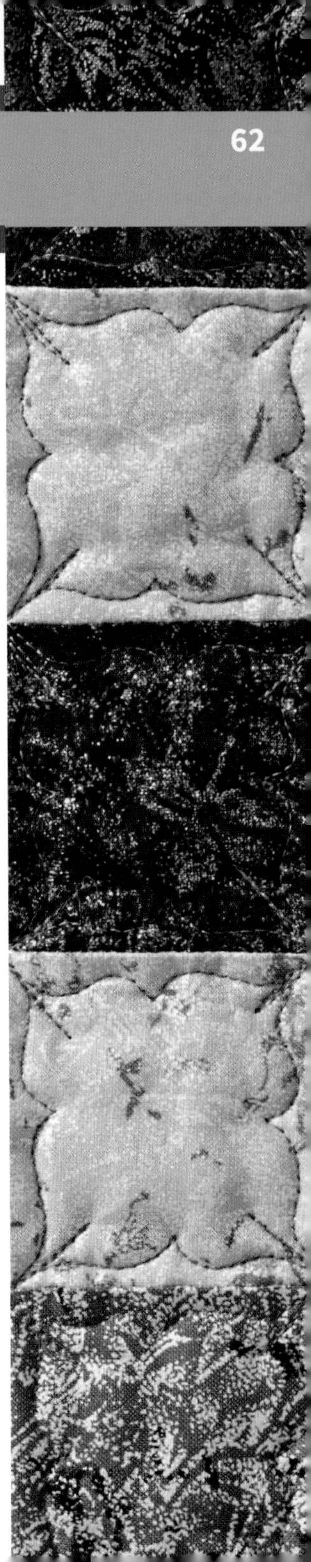

PRACTICE

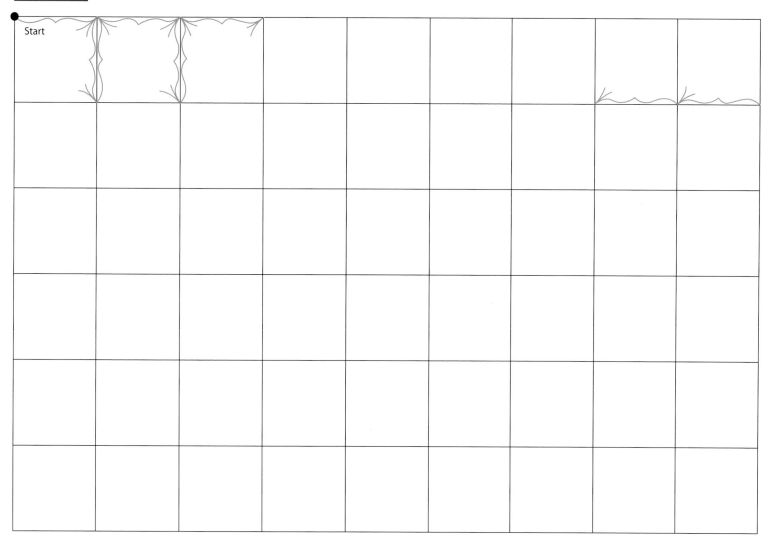

Start

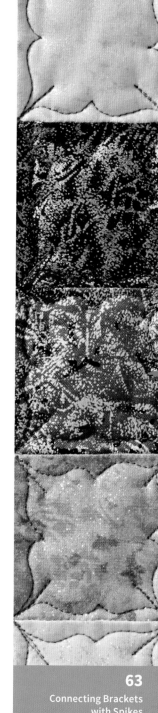

TALK YOURSELF THROUGH THE DESIGN.

First line of design: Over • Spike • Spike • Down • Spike • Spike • Up • Spike • Spike. Repeat to the end of the row.

Second line of design: Over • Spike • Spike • Over • Spike • Spike. Return to the first square in the row.

Repeat the first and second lines of the design to fill the entire practice grid.

When the grid is filled, the last line of the design (or exit path) is Up • Spike • Spike • Up • Spike • Spike • Up • Spike • Spike, all the way back to the starting point.

BORDER GRID LAYOUT 1

Stitch inside the grid, this time with a single spike.

Stitch outside the grid, adding 1 spike whenever the squares meet.

Combine both passes.

Start

Start

Start

BORDER GRID LAYOUT 2

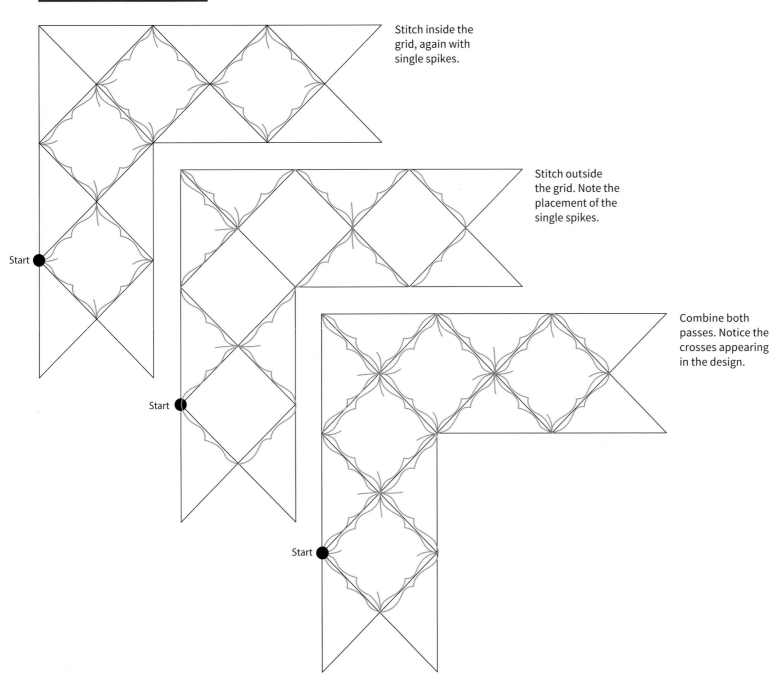

Stitch inside the grid, again with single spikes.

Stitch outside the grid. Note the placement of the single spikes.

Combine both passes. Notice the crosses appearing in the design.

Start

Start

Start

At this point you have mastered the continuous flow of a stitched design within the basic four-patch and border squares set on point. Next, we turn our attention to blocks that include irregular shapes. These demand a slightly different strategy. The clockwise direction, however, remains at the core of executing the continuous stitching method.

The next level of difficulty involves planning an exit strategy using the points of intersection to diverge into and capture areas of a block. It also involves developing an eye for mapping a travel path that will lead you from area to area. These complex blocks take more thought to execute a continuous quilting strategy, but over time they will become second nature. Remember, each quilter will stitch their block differently. The guidelines given here will help you find your own individual strategy.

Some tools that will help you in this section are a lightbox; a dry-erase marker and a clear vinyl overlay (such as Premium Clear Vinyl by C&T Publishing); or simply a window, tracing paper, and a pencil. Keep in mind that blocks are stabilized first and then filled with continuous-line designs—without the need to stop and restart your thread. We will address how this is done after we discuss design strategies within blocks.

Let's begin by building on what you already know.

BLOCK 1

In keeping with your practice grid exercises, the clockwise stitching path of this Twenty-Five–Patch block will be very familiar. The twist comes at the last intersection of the first row (see the first red dot). At this point you can move into the square in the row below to capture and complete the lone square of row 2, and then return to row 1 and complete it. The importance of the intersection becomes apparent—at intersections you can veer into other nearby sections of the block. Finish numbering the stitching sequence. Notice the solid red line, your exit path. Just as in your practice grid, this path remains unstitched until you are ready to return to the starting point.

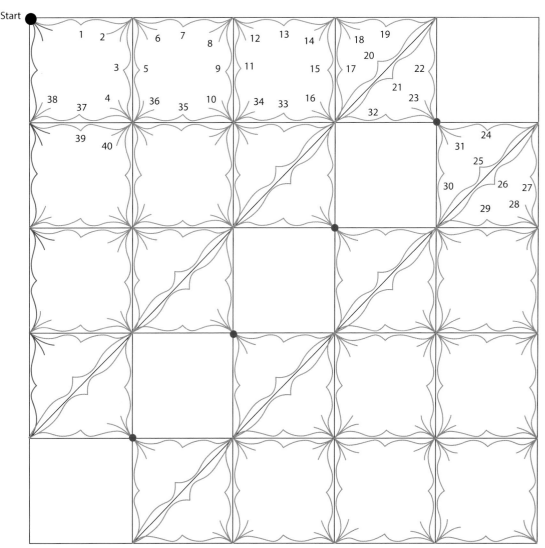

Refer to Connecting Brackets with Spikes (page 62).

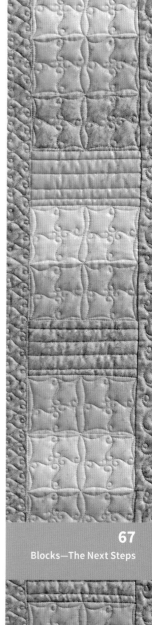

BLOCK 2

Let's look more closely at travel paths. Irregular blocks may sometimes require a travel path to assist in the continuous movement around the shapes. A travel path passes through the block, intentionally leaving other design lines unstitched (these are completed later). Notice how 1, 2, 3, and 4 take you across the top of the row to the furthest block. Return through those blocks, completing the first row, by following 5 through 17.

Work each row as you have done before, always being conscious of your travel path and your exit path (the solid red line). The stars are fillers, meaning you start and end the design at the same point. Pause, stitch the stars whenever you come to them, and then continue along your path. Complete this block, drawing dashed lines for your travel paths and numbering the stitching segments.

Refer to Connecting Curves with Spikes (page 26).

BLOCK 3

Begin this next nine-patch by stitching-in-the-ditch around the outside of the block, adding the bottom left rose petal as you go. Because this stitching design is symmetrical and consistent, always beginning and ending at the same point, we need a travel path. Without a travel path we would be stuck after completing the design in each half-square triangle. The travel path will allow us to work row by row, keeping the far left-hand side partially unfinished as our exit path.

Travel paths are shown here as a dashed line. It may help to think of using a travel path to "reach" over to the last block of each row. Complete areas as you move back to the left; then travel through the first block of each row and down to the next row. Make the filler rose petals at any point, but make sure to do so *before* you leave those intersections.

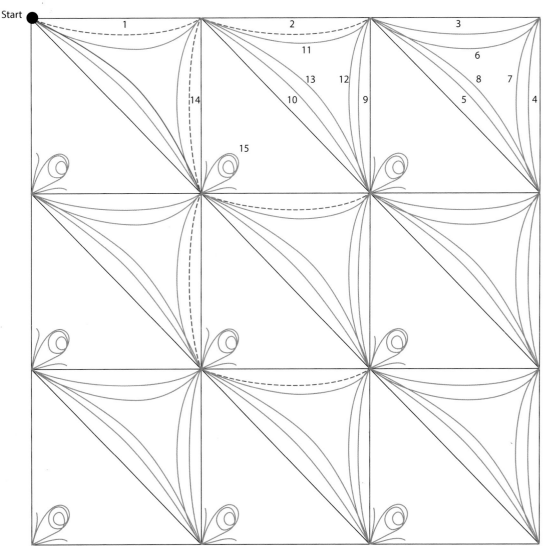

Refer to Connecting Curves with Petals (page 22).

BLOCK 4

Next we will examine a series of Nine-Patch blocks where the exit path is less obvious. Even though the nine-patch is comprised of familiar shapes, such as four-patches and half-square triangles, how do you get from space to space? The challenge is to plan your continuous stitching to capture all the shapes and exit through the top left.

The path is numbered to get you started; your exit path is given. Notice the progression of the four-patch in the top right corner. Instead of top left, you enter the four-patch bottom left. Don't panic. Pick up the pattern you know from your four-patch exercises and you will exit the block where you came in. Remember, these are suggested routes designed to help train your eye to find a path for overall execution. Try different paths by using clear vinyl and a dry-erase marker or a lightbox and tracing paper. Number your path.

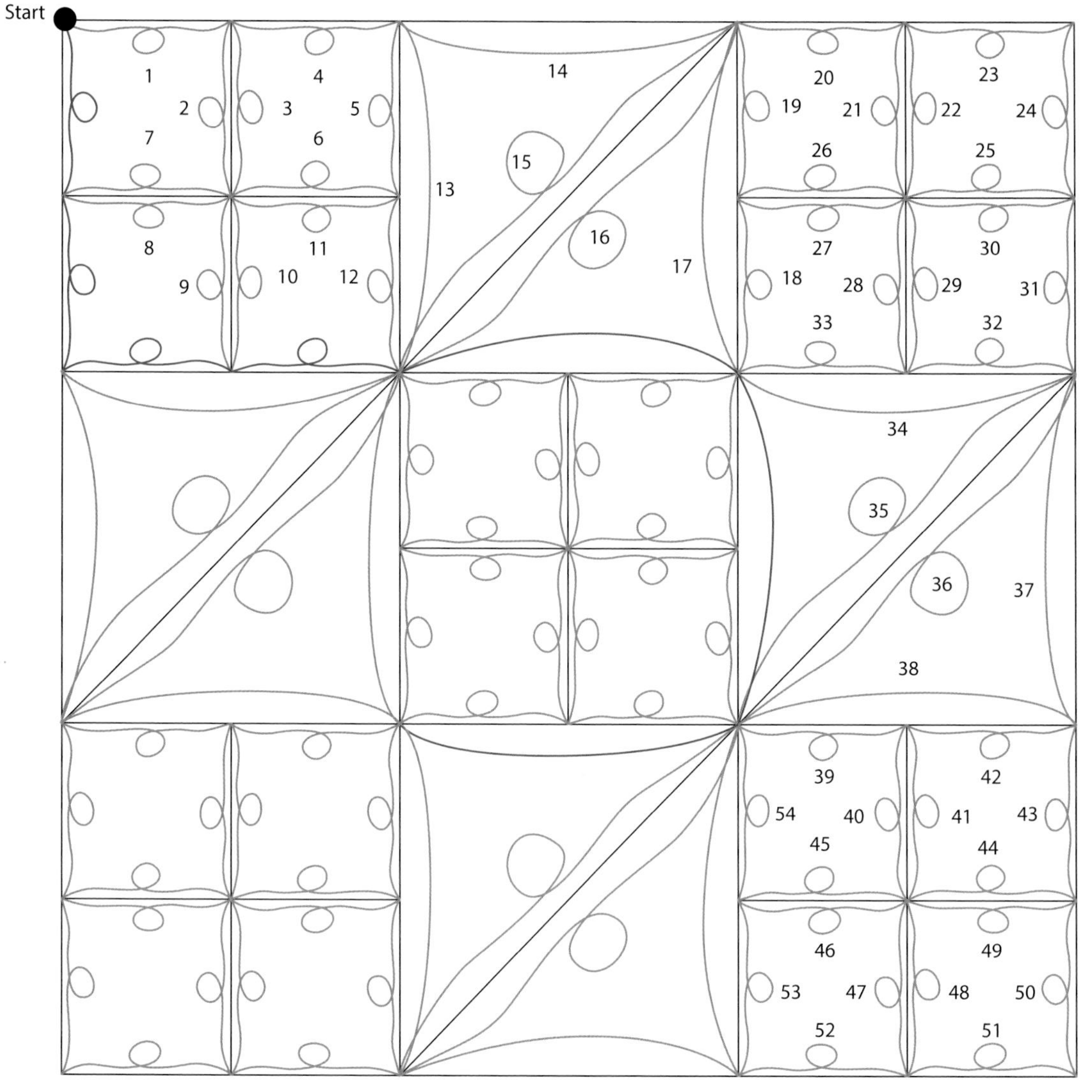

Start

Refer to Connecting Loops (page 42).

BLOCK 5

This is a variation of the previous nine-patch. Only the final exit path is shown in red. Mark where your travel paths will be, if any, and where to extend your exit path, if needed. Then number the block the way you would execute the stitching design. Keep in mind that your travel direction is always clockwise within each shape. If you want to challenge yourself, use the clear vinyl overlay and try entering the Four-Patch blocks from various corners.

Start

Refer to Connecting Curl 1 (page 46).

BLOCK 6

Follow the numbers to understand the continuous-line strategy in this block. Ask yourself, "Which areas are completed entirely? Which design lines are left open, and why?" Notice the simple path in and out of the corner four-patches that mimics your practice of border designs with squares set on point (see Basic Connecting Designs, page 18). Fill in the numbers to complete the path. Work in a *clockwise* direction around the block.

....

Tip • If you lose track of where you are going, stop at an intersection with your needle down; then continue quilting when you have confirmed where to go next. And remember your clockwise direction!

....

Refer to Connecting Curves with Leaves (pages 30).

BLOCK 7

Think about the last three Nine-Patch blocks. What do they have in common? Notice how the design is stitched initially in the upper left-hand corner until it arrives at the top left corner of the center square. At that intersection, the perimeter of the central square is used as an exit path.

In this nine-patch, however, the perimeter of the central square becomes a travel path. At crucial points, the line captures and completes neighboring areas, always returning to the inside travel path. Then, just as in the previous nine-patches, any remaining designs in the central square are stitched before exiting the block.

Is there another way to stitch this block? Notice that at times you may *think* you are moving in a counter-clockwise direction (center square); however, take a second look. Within the smaller shape you are completing a segment of the design and indeed moving in a clockwise direction! At each intersection, pause and remind yourself to move clockwise in that space.

Refer to Connecting Curl 2 (page 50) and Connecting Brackets (page 58).

BLOCK 8

Based on the strategy revealed in the previous nine-patch, provide the stitching sequence numbers. The travel and exit paths are given. Would you have chosen different travel paths? Complete the innermost curves and filler curls last before exiting.

Refer to Connecting Curves with Curls (page 34).

BLOCK 9

In this variation of a nine-patch, the star itself provides the travel path. Stitching-in-the-ditch can get you from one area to the next. Fillers are a great way to pause, fill in an area, and pick up where you left off. *Hint:* In the corner squares, stitch the curls first, then the curves.

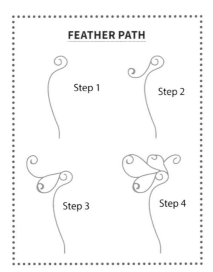

FEATHER PATH

Step 1

Step 2

Step 3

Step 4

Start

Refer to Connecting Curl 2 (page 50) and Connecting Double Curls (page 54).

BLOCK 10

The next four blocks do not have a starting point in the top left corner. At first glance, this next block may seem daunting—but don't let the starting point throw you. Instead, ask yourself the basic questions about fillers, intersections, and where your travel and exit paths are. Which areas have to be completed when you come to them? Remember the crucial intersection (see the red dot) where you reach the top left corner of the center block. That is the point you start moving into different areas. Use your vinyl overlay to complete the design in a continuous line.

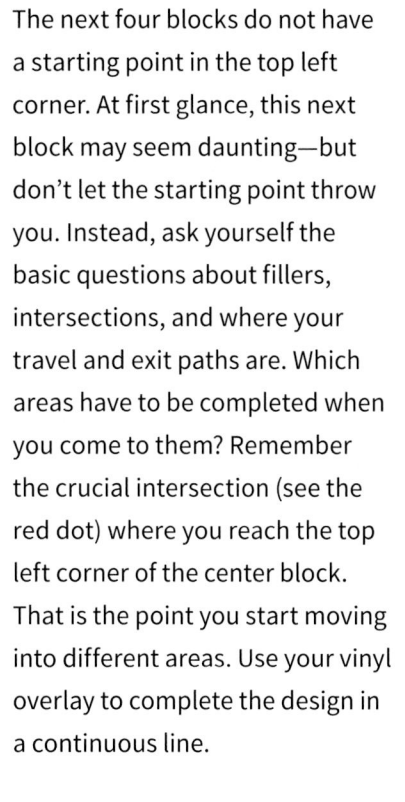

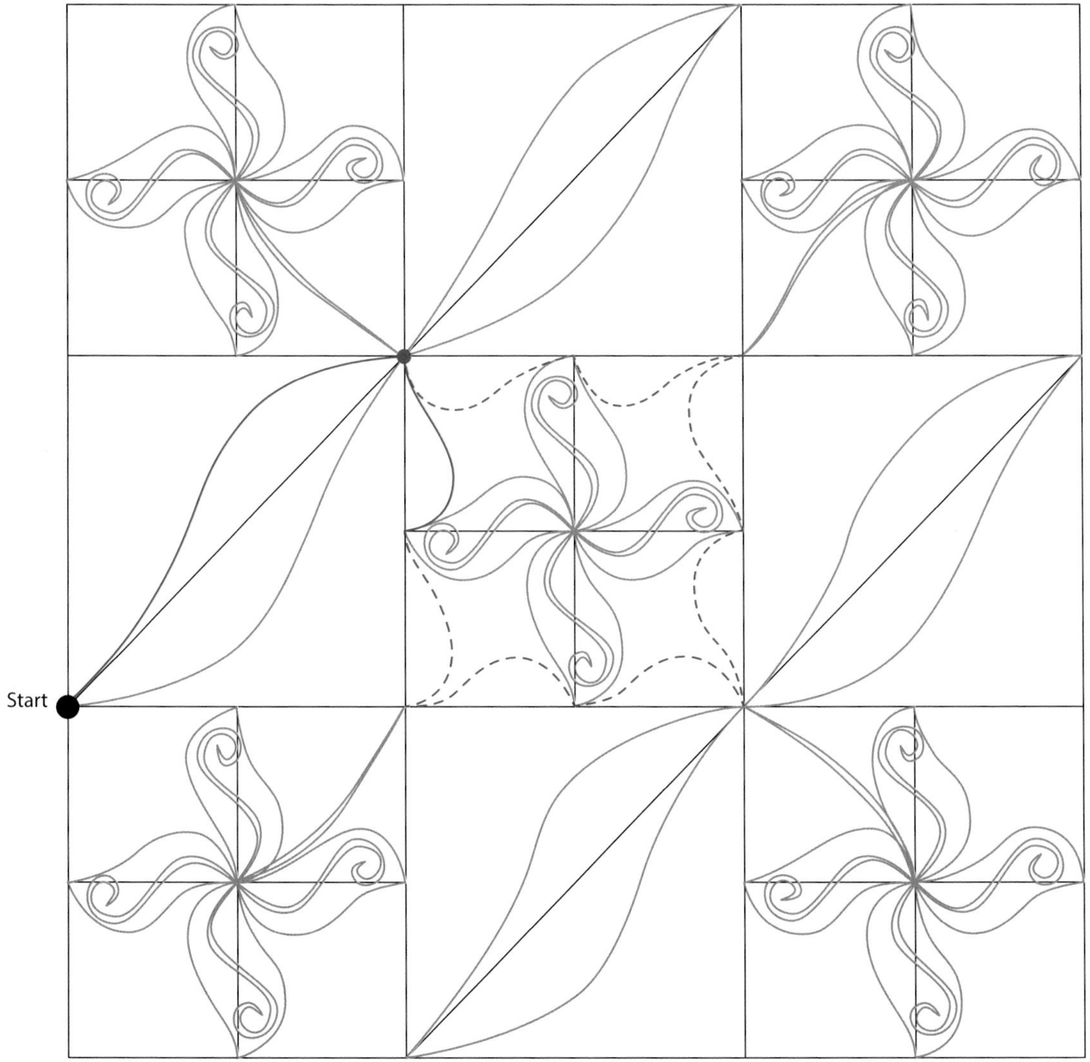

Refer to Connecting Waves (page 38).

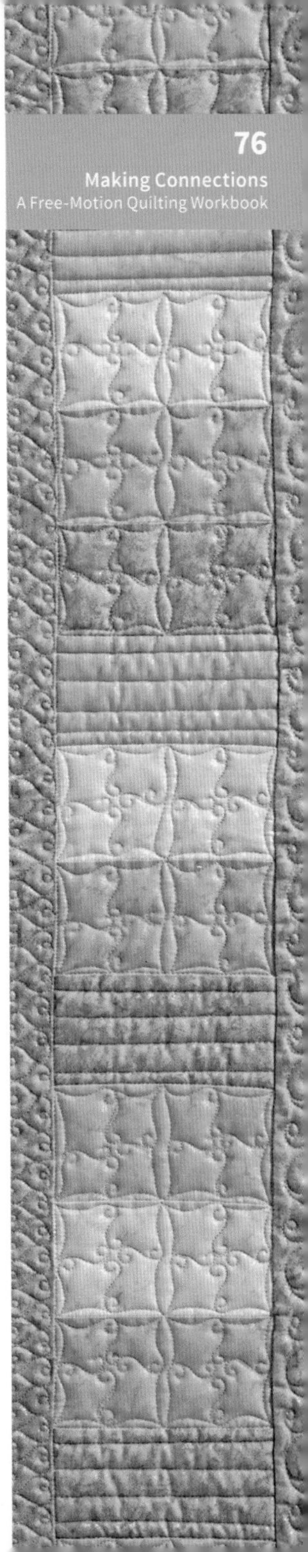

BLOCK 11

Follow the stitching sequence. Notice how it detours and completes the large feather plume in the Flying Geese before a corner block is completed (see 4 and 5, 14 and 15). As we've seen in previous blocks, the outside lines of the center square serve as the travel path to move around and capture each neighboring space. Note that the large feathers never touch the travel path. Because of this, and the fact that they are fillers, the large feathers must be completed during the stitching of the corner squares.

By the way, if you feel like you are moving counterclockwise (39–53), look again. Within each of the smaller shapes you are actually completing the stitching design clockwise! Move in a clockwise direction. It's the golden rule! In this block, try to incorporate some of your own embellishments in the Flying Geese and still keep your line going.

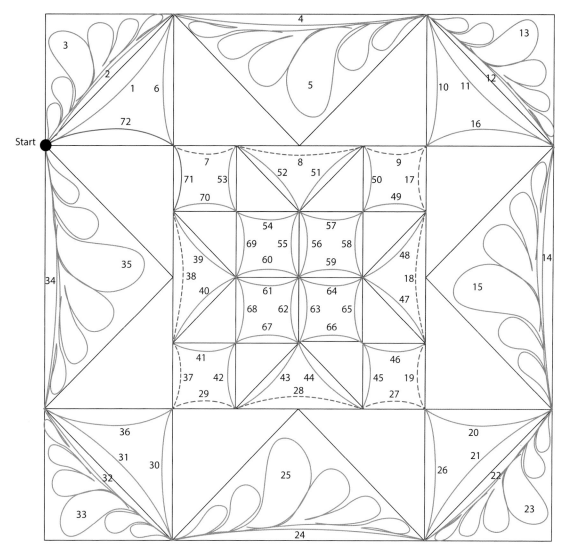

Refer to Basic Connecting Designs (page 18).

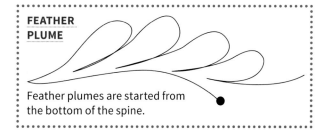

FEATHER PLUME

Feather plumes are started from the bottom of the spine.

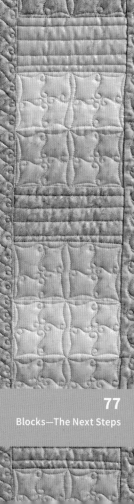

BLOCK 12

Study the stitching strategy of this block. It completes similar elements first, second, and third, and involves two travel paths (the dashed and dotted lines). First you will stitch the rose petals and long arcs (4 and 5). The first travel path (the dashed line) is used to reach those designs. Second, the outer squares' curves are added using the second travel path (the dotted line) to reach each space. Complete the filler spikes for the center along this second travel path. Use a clear vinyl overlay and dry-erase marker to try different ways of moving around the block. Always maintain the clockwise direction. *Hint:* Don't let it throw you that you reach the starting point before finishing the block. Think of this starting point as an intersection.

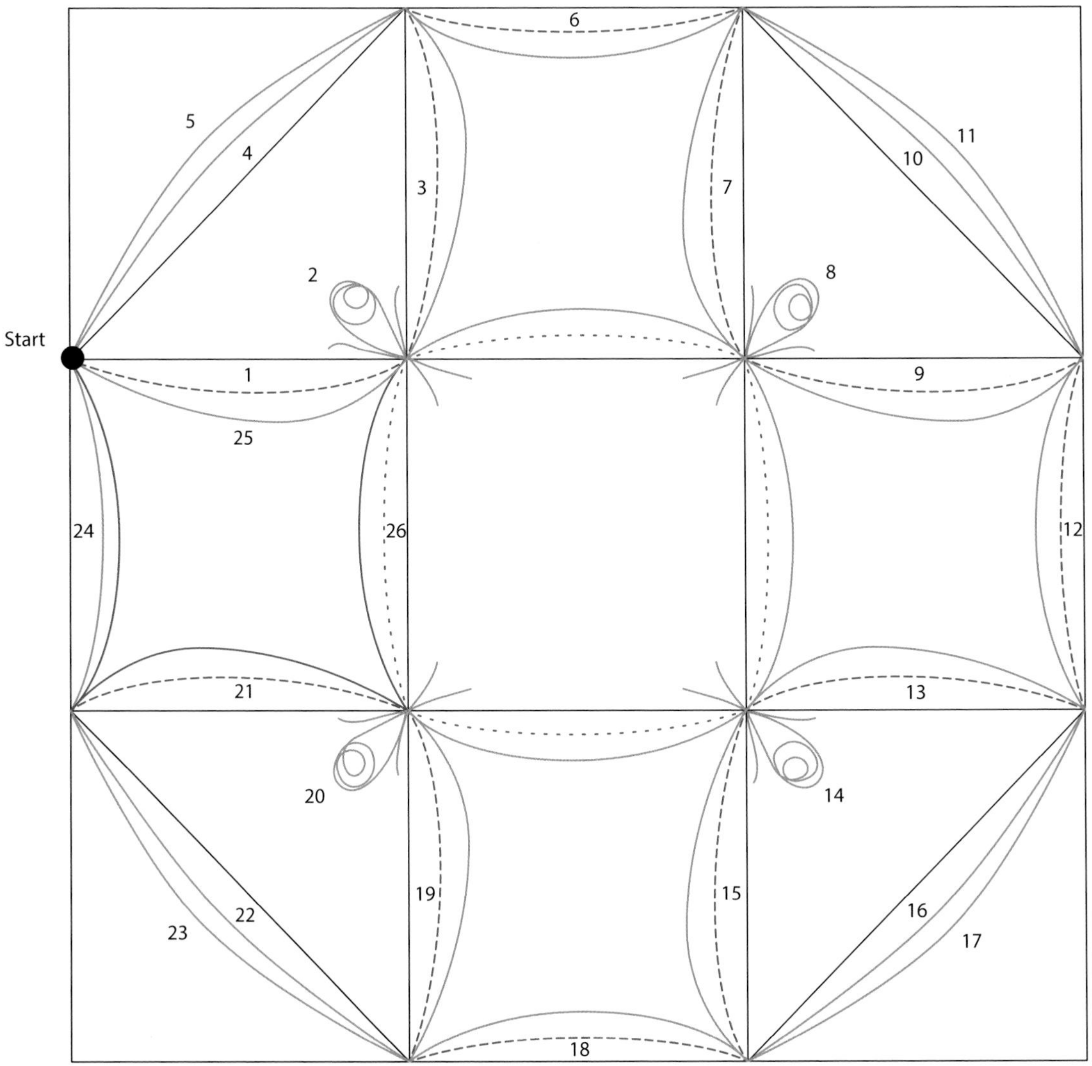

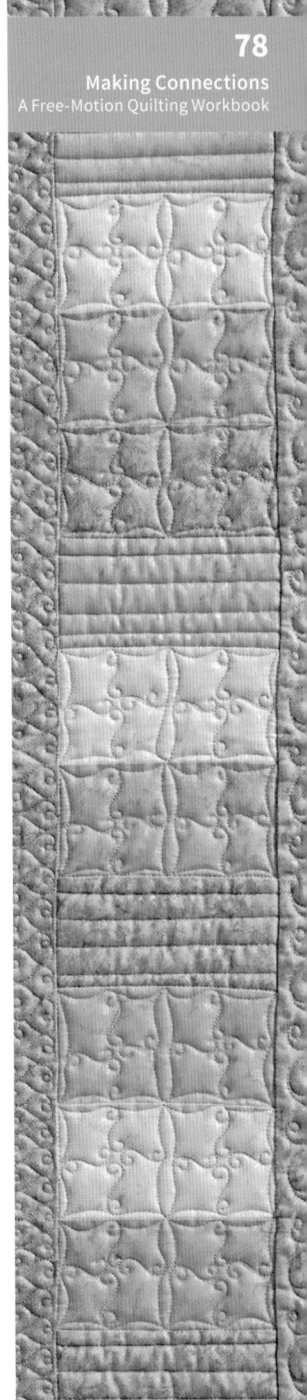

Refer to Connecting Curves with Petals (pages 22).

BLOCK 13

Analyze this block. There are strategies here you have seen before. Look for the filler designs. What intersections can or must you use to access them? Use the vinyl overlay to mark the crucial intersections with a dot. At which points will you be stuck if you complete a design? Where can you go instead?

Lines 10 and 11 are travel paths helping you to reach the top left corner of the center square. A portion of the exit path is given. Is the path around the center square a travel or an exit path? Ask yourself basic questions to guide your eye and find your continuous line. Number the sequence that you would follow. Remember to always travel clockwise.

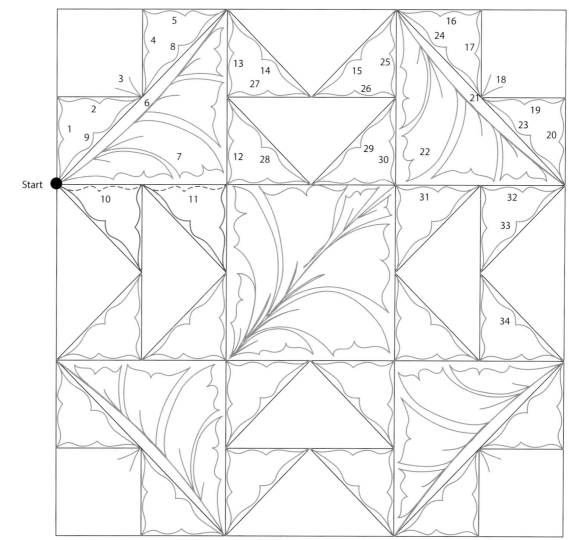

Refer to Connecting Brackets (page 58).

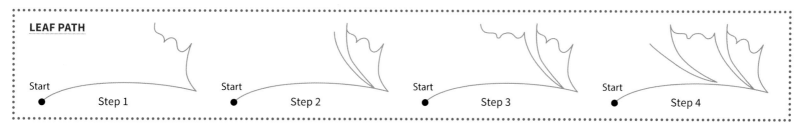

LEAF PATH

Start — Step 1

Start — Step 2

Start — Step 3

Start — Step 4

BLOCK 14

This Nine-Patch block is partially numbered to get you started. Do you recognize any elements you've tackled before? Which areas do you need to reach and complete first? Will you need travel paths? Is the stitching path around the center square a travel path or an exit path? Feel free to change the numbering to accommodate your stitching. Use a clear vinyl overlay with dry-erase markers to map your continuous stitching strategy. If you get stuck, erase and start again. With each try, a clear travel path and exit path will develop.

Refer to Connecting Curl 2 (page 50), Connecting Double Curls (page 54), and Feather Path (page 75).

BLOCK 15

This final block comprises several shapes and designs you are familiar with. A numbering sequence has already been started for you. Which areas will you complete first? Second? Third? How will you travel around the block? Where is your exit path? Use your dry-erase marker and clear vinyl overlay to devise a strategy.

....

Tip • If you miss a section of the block, simply place a flat-head pin in that spot and come back to stitch it later.
....

Refer to Connecting Curves with Petals (page 22) and Feather Plume (page 77).

Quilting Direction

Horizontal Quilt without Sashing

Always stitch-in-the-ditch around a block first, and then, without stopping and starting your thread again, stitch the inside block designs. In order to keep the continuous line going, you may have to stitch the block design before every side of the block has been completely stabilized with stitching. Note that in some cases you may enter a block at the top right. In the first row of this quilt, you would stitch blocks 1, 3, and 2. The second row blocks are stitched in order from left to right; the third row is similar to the second. Advance the quilt between quilting the rows.

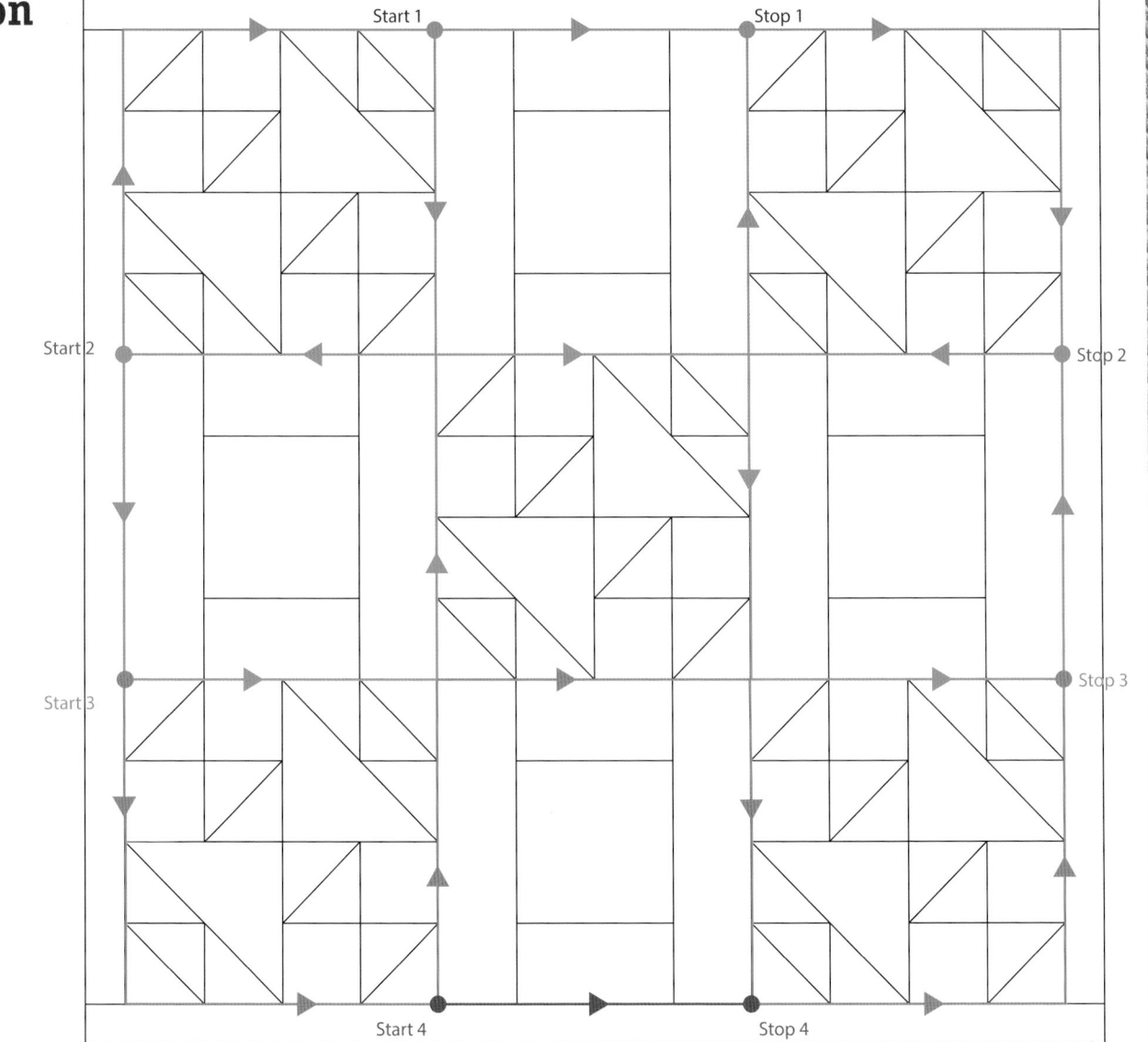

Quilting Direction

Horizontal Quilt with Sashing

Study the stitch-in-the-ditch paths. At what points would you pause and complete the blocks? The sashing?

Note

Reasons why you might have to make an unintentional stop:

1. Broke thread
2. Backed into a corner
3. Missed a section
4. Stitched the wrong design
5. Emptied bobbin

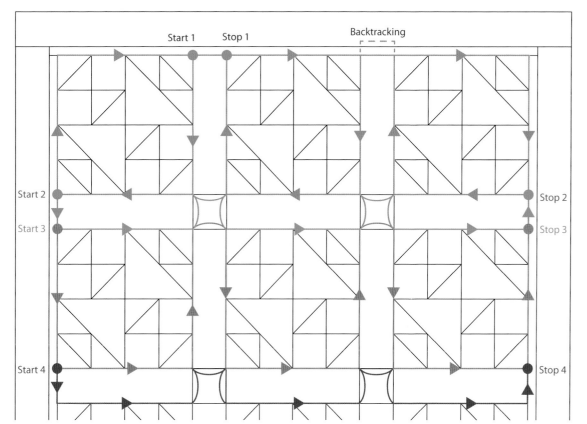

Sunshine and Lemon Drops

Finished block: 8″ × 8″ • **Finished quilt:** 50″ × 50″

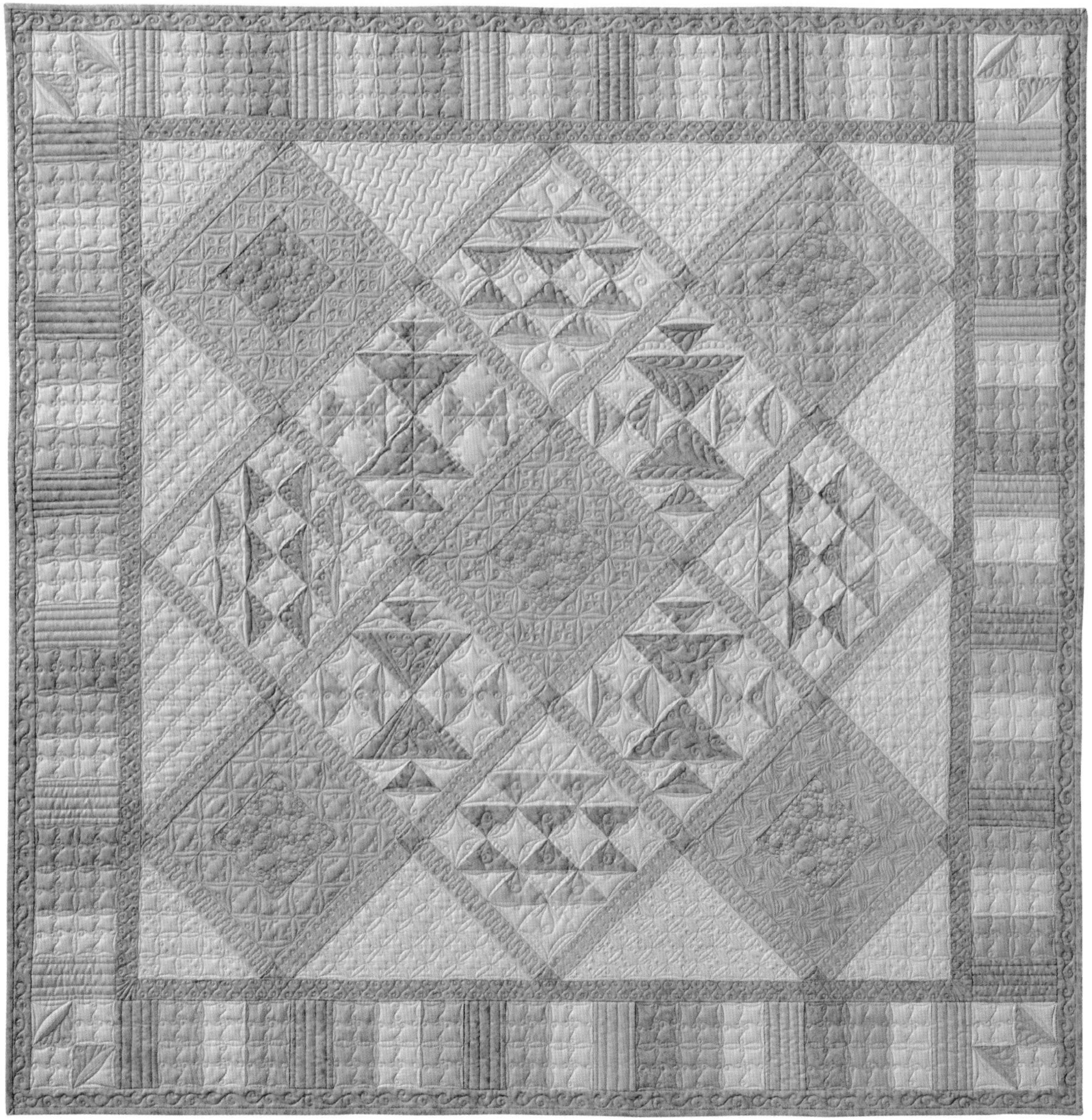

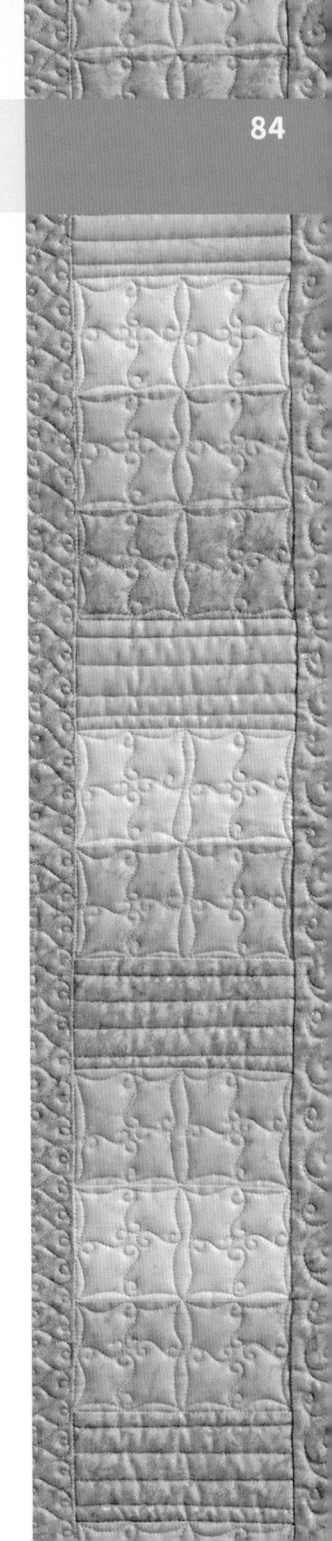

Fabric Requirements

Fabrics from the Fairy Frost collection by Michael Miller Fabrics were used in the sample quilt.

All yardage is based on 42″-wide fabric.

(A) Turquoise (Fairy Frost Luna): 1⅝ yards (includes 15″ for binding)

(B) Green (Fairy Frost Fresh): ¾ yard

(C) Yellow (Fairy Frost Maize): ¾ yard

(D) Cream (Fairy Frost Rice): 1⅓ yards

Backing: 3¼ yards of cream (Fairy Frost Rice)

Batting: 56″ × 56″

Cutting Instructions

Turquoise (A)

- Cut 1 strip 6″ × width of fabric; subcut into 4 squares 6″ × 6″ for the half-square triangles.

  From the rest of the strip, cut 2 strips 1½″ wide; subcut into 24 squares 1½″ × 1½″ for the cornerstones.

- Cut 1 strip 4⅞″ × width of fabric; subcut into 4 squares 4⅞″ × 4⅞″. Cut on the diagonal once to make 8 triangles for block 2.

8 triangles

- Cut 2 strips 4½″ × width of fabric; subcut into 5 squares 4½″ × 4½″ for block 1 and 20 rectangles 2½″ × 4½″ for the piano-key border.

- Cut 6 strips 2½″ × width of fabric for the binding.

Always measure your actual quilt before cutting border strips to size.

- Cut 9 strips 1½″ × width of fabric. Piece together 5 strips; subcut into 2 strips 1½″ × 48½″ and 2 strips 1½″ × 50½″ for the outer border. Piece together the remaining 4 strips; subcut into 2 strips 1½″ × 38½″ and 2 strips 1½″ × 40½″ for the inner border.

Green (B)

- Cut 1 strip 6″ × width of fabric; subcut into 5 squares 6″ × 6″ for the half-square triangles.

- Cut 6 strips 2½″ × width of fabric; subcut into 10 rectangles 2½″ × 8½″ for block 1 and 30 rectangles 2½″ × 4½″ for the piano-key border and block 1.

Yellow (C)

- Cut 2 strips 4½″ × width of fabric; subcut into 20 rectangles 2½″ × 4½″ for the piano-key border.

- Cut 9 strips 1½″ × width of fabric; subcut into 36 rectangles 1½″ × 8½″ for the sashing.

Cream (D)

- Cut 1 strip 12⅝″ × width of fabric; subcut into 2 squares 12⅝″ × 12⅝″. Cut on the diagonal twice to make 8 setting triangles.

8 setting triangles

  From the rest of the strip, cut 2 squares 6⅝″ × 6⅝″. Cut on the diagonal once to make 4 corner triangles.

4 corner triangles

- Cut 2 strips 6″ × width of fabric; subcut into 9 squares 6″ × 6″ for the half-square triangles.

  From the rest of the strip, cut 1 strip 2⅞″ wide; subcut into 8 squares 2⅞″ × 2⅞″. Cut each square on the diagonal once to make 16 triangles for block 2.

16 triangles

- Cut 2 strips 4½″ × width of fabric; subcut into 20 rectangles 2½″ × 4½″ for the piano-key border.

- Cut 3 strips 2½″ wide; subcut into 48 squares 2½″ × 2½″ for the blocks.

Making the Blocks

Half-Square Triangles

1. On the wrong side of a 6″ × 6″ cream (D) square, draw diagonal lines from corner to corner in both directions.

2. Place the 6″ × 6″ cream (D) square right sides together with a 6″ × 6″ turquoise (A) square.

3. Stitch ¼″ on both sides of each diagonal line.

4. Without moving the fabric, make 4 cuts: from top to bottom and side to side through the center, and on both diagonals. Press to the turquoise and trim to 2½″. You will have 8 half-square triangles.

5. Repeat Steps 1–4 to make a total of 32 turquoise/cream (A/D) half-square triangles and 40 green/cream (B/D) half-square triangles.

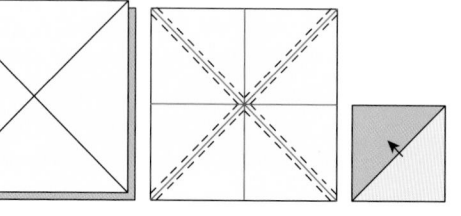

Four-Patches

1. Sew a green/cream (B/D) half-square triangle to a cream (D) 2½″ × 2½″ square, as shown. Press towards the cream (D) square. Make 2.

2. Sew 2 of these units together to make a four-patch.

3. Repeat Steps 1 and 2 to make a total of 12 four-patches. The blocks should measure 4½″ square.

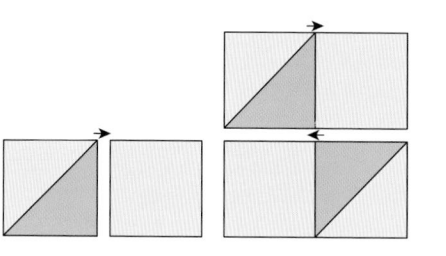

Block 1

1. Sew 2 green (B) 2½″ × 4½″ rectangles to opposite sides of the center turquoise (A) 4½″ × 4½″ square. Press toward the green rectangles.

2. Sew 2 green (B) 2½″ × 8½″ rectangles to the top and bottom of the unit from Step 1. Press toward the green rectangles.

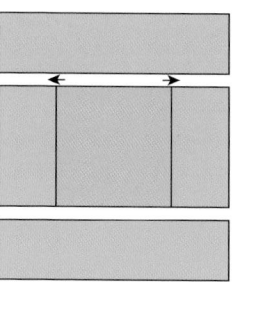

3. Repeat Steps 1 and 2 to make a total of 5 blocks. The blocks should measure 8½″ × 8½″.

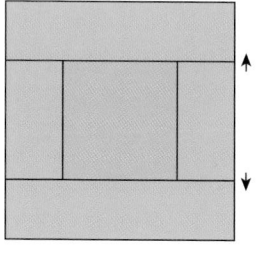

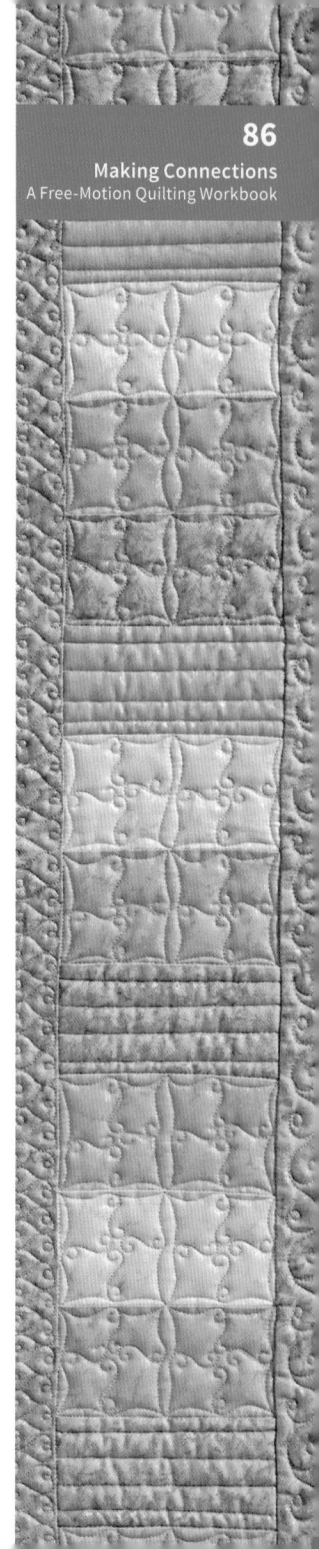

Block 2

1. Sew 2 cream (D) 2⅞″ triangles to the sides of a turquoise/cream (A/D) half-square triangle to make a larger triangle. Press toward the cream (D) triangle. Make 2.

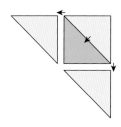

2. Sew this unit to the long edge of a turquoise (A) 4⅞″ triangle. Press toward the turquoise triangle. Make 2. These blocks should measure 4½″ × 4½″.

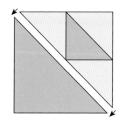

3. Finish sewing the block together as shown, using 2 of the green/cream (B/D) four-patches. Press as shown.

4. Repeat Steps 1–3 to make a total of 4 blocks. The blocks should measure 8½″ × 8½″.

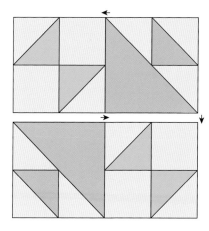

Block 3

1. Select 4 green/cream (B/D) half-square triangles. Re-press the seams of 2 squares toward the cream (D) fabric.

2. Select 6 turquoise/cream (A/D) half-square triangles. Re-press the seam allowance of 2 squares toward the cream (D) fabric.

3. Arrange and sew the half-square triangle units and 6 cream (D) 2½″ × 2½″ squares together as shown; press according to the arrows.

4. Repeat Steps 1–3 to make a total of 4 blocks. The blocks should measure 8½″ × 8½″.

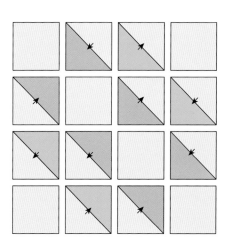

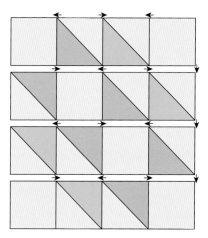

Quilt Assembly

Sashing

1. Sew 2 turquoise (A) 1½″ × 1½″ squares to each end of a yellow (C) 1½″ × 8½″ sashing strip; press toward the sashing. Make 2. *Fig. A*

2. Sew 4 turquoise (A) 1½″ × 1½″ squares to 3 yellow (C) 1½″ × 8½″ sashing strips; press toward the sashing. Make 2. *Fig. B*

3. Sew 6 turquoise (A) 1½″ × 1½″ squares to 5 yellow (C) 1½″ × 8½″ sashing strips; press toward the sashing. Make 2. *Fig. C*

4. Join the blocks, sashing, setting triangles, and corner triangles in diagonal rows, as shown. Press toward the sashing. Trim the cornerstones and setting triangles as necessary to create a straight edge. The quilt center should measure 38½″ × 38½″.

A.

B.

C.

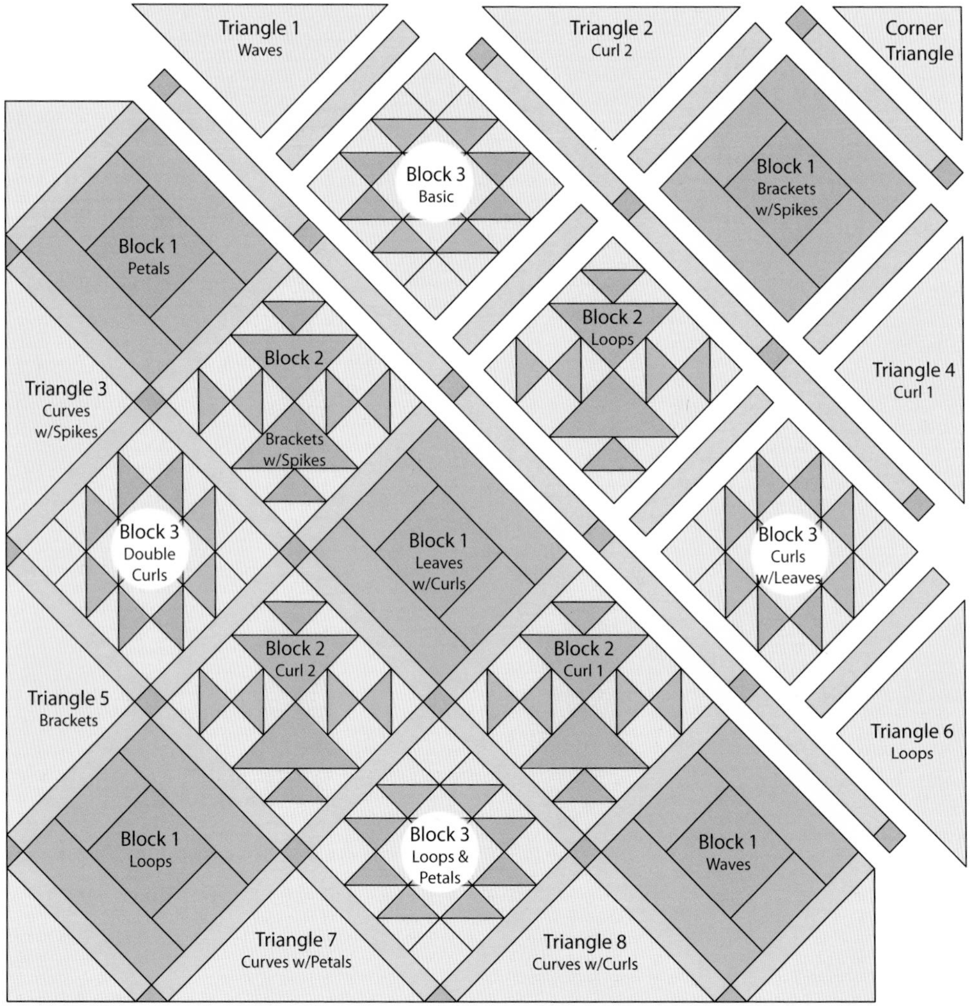

Triangle 1
Waves

Triangle 2
Curl 2

Corner
Triangle

Block 3
Basic

Block 1
Brackets
w/Spikes

Block 1
Petals

Block 2
Loops

Block 2

Brackets
w/Spikes

Triangle 3
Curves
w/Spikes

Triangle 4
Curl 1

Block 3
Double
Curls

Block 1
Leaves
w/Curls

Block 3
Curls
w/Leaves

Block 2
Curl 2

Block 2
Curl 1

Triangle 5
Brackets

Block 1
Loops

Block 3
Loops &
Petals

Block 1
Waves

Triangle 6
Loops

Triangle 7
Curves w/Petals

Triangle 8
Curves w/Curls

Quilt assembly

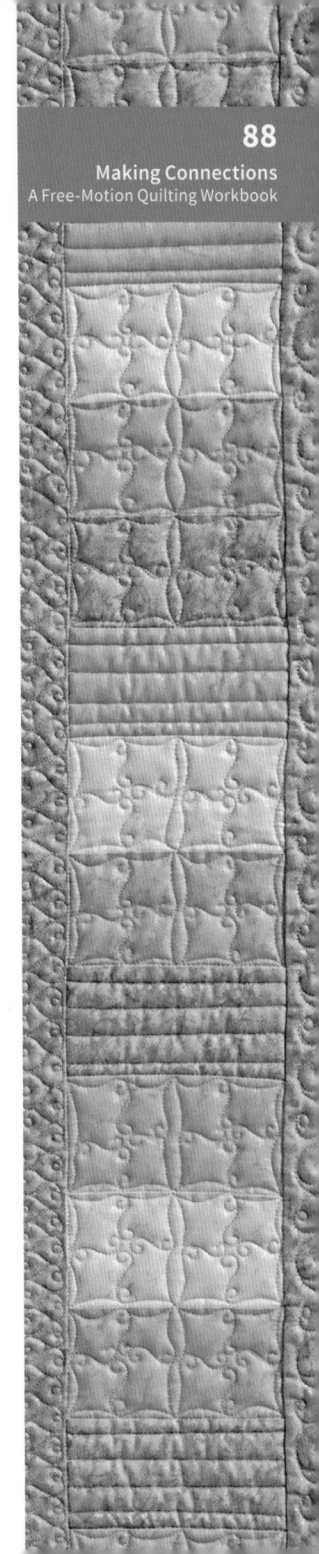

Inner Border

1. Sew the 38½″ turquoise (A) border strips to the sides of the quilt center; press toward the inner border.

2. Sew the 40½″ turquoise (A) border strips to the top and bottom of the quilt center; press toward the inner border.

Piano-Key Border

1. Piece together 20 rectangles 2½″ × 4½″, 5 from each color, in the order shown in the diagram: A, B, D, C, A, B, D, C.

Repeat to make a total of 4 border strips. The border strips should measure 40½″ long. Adjust a few seams a bit as needed.

2. Sew 2 piano-key borders to the sides of the quilt center. Press to the inner border.

3. Add corner block four-patches to each end of the 2 remaining piano-key borders. Sew these to the top and bottom of the quilt center. Press to the inner border.

Outer Border

1. Sew the 48½″ turquoise (A) border strips to the sides of the quilt center; press toward the outer border.

2. Sew the 50½″ turquoise (A) border strips to the top and bottom of the quilt center; press toward the outer border.

Finishing the Quilt

1. Layer the top, batting, and backing.

2. Quilt.

The following chapter gives you ideas and guidance for quilting this quilt. You will notice that I have combined and modified the quilting designs from this book in fun and creative ways to give you ideas and inspiration. For instance, the corner setting triangles (page 109) have been quilted in curls (page 50) with alternate rows done in simple curves (page 18). Note also the turquoise inner and outer borders and yellow sashing— continuous motifs (page 91) fit perfectly in these narrower areas. As for the piano-key border, I simply treated the rectangles as though they were 2 blocks of a four-patch. With marking chalk and a ruler, I divided the border rectangles in half and quilted using a double curl (page 54). You should feel free to modify the quilting any way you think will be perfect for *your* quilt.

3. Bind using the 2½″ turquoise (A) binding strips.

Quilting Direction

Quilt on Point

Now that your quilt top is completed, it's time to use all that you've learned to quilt it. The first step is to stitch-in-the-ditch, stabilizing row by row as you complete blocks, setting triangles, and corners as you go. Study these diagrams and plan to interrupt your stitching-in-the-ditch to complete these areas. Stitching suggestions for all corresponding blocks and triangles are given to you on the following pages. Refer to the quilt assembly diagram (page 88). The idea is to stabilize the blocks or triangles as much as possible before quilting in them.

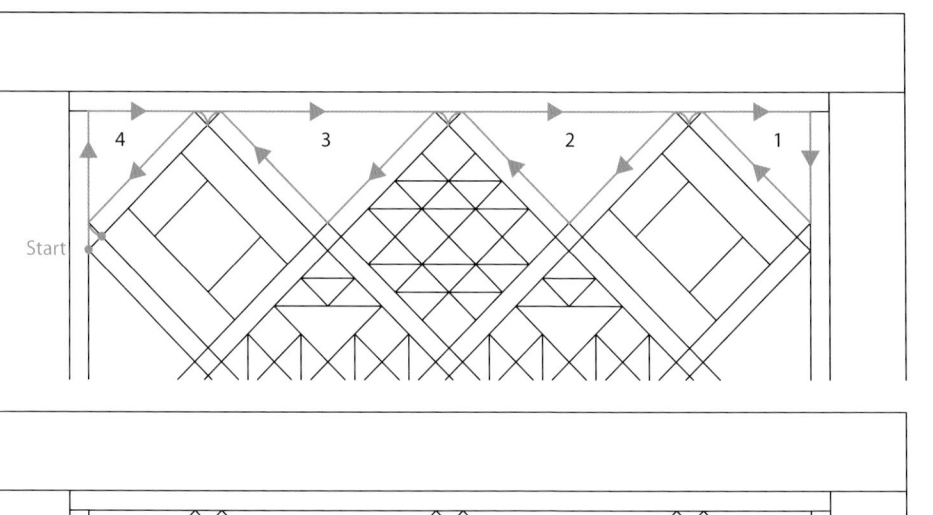

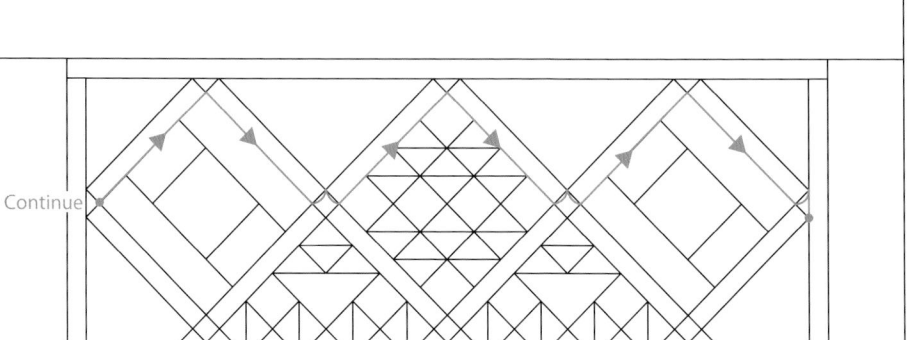

Stitch-in-the-ditch around the block. Then continue stitching the inside block designs.

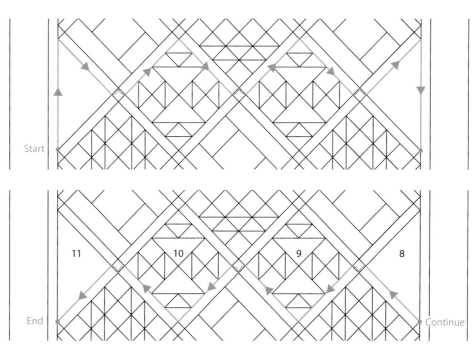

Start

End   Continue

11   10   9   8

Continue to work the remaining rows of the quilt in this fashion.

In addition, continuous-line designs can be added to the sashing. These would be usable designs for the inner and outer borders, as well.

Block 1: Petals

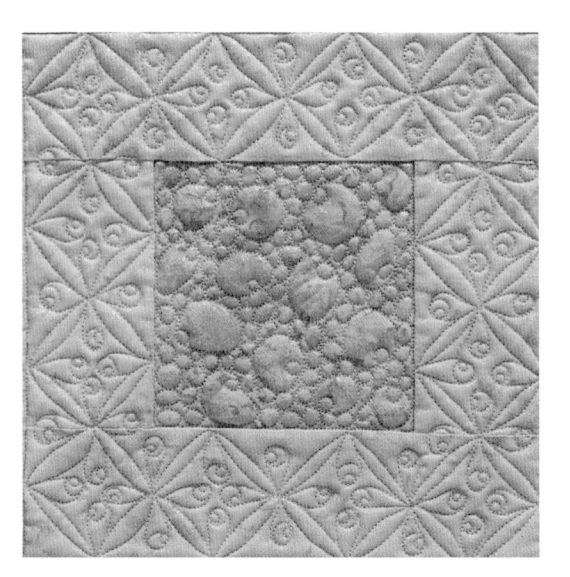

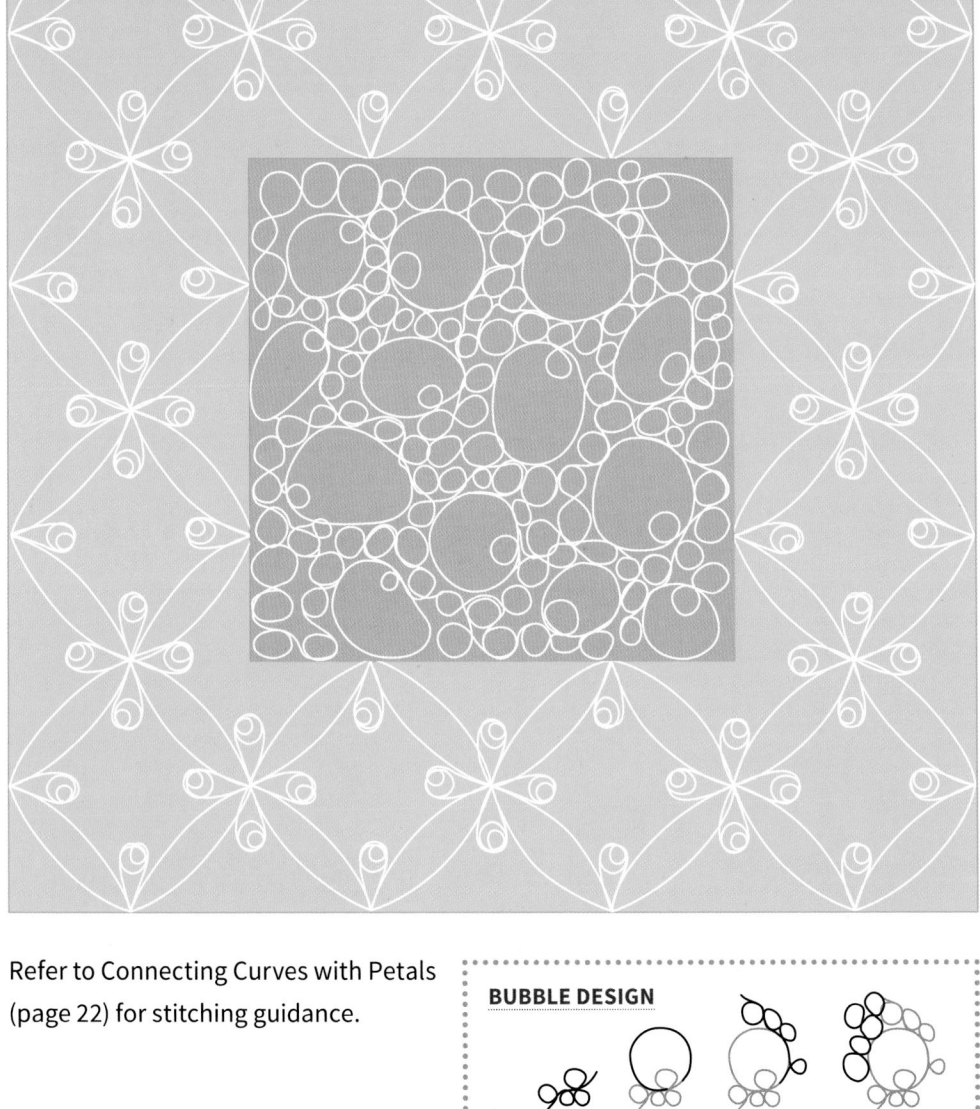

Refer to Connecting Curves with Petals (page 22) for stitching guidance.

BUBBLE DESIGN

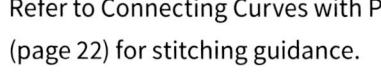

Start

Block 1: Bracket with Spikes

Refer to Connecting Brackets with Spikes (page 62) and Bubble Design (page 92) for stitching guidance.

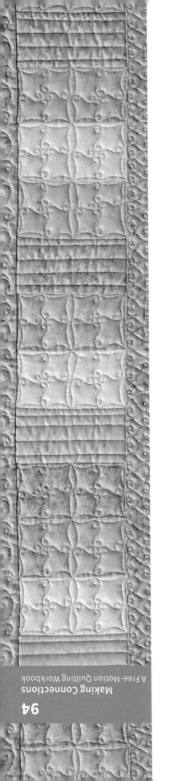

Refer to Connecting Curves with Curls (page 34), adding a leaf at the intersections, and Bubble Design (page 92) for stitching guidance.

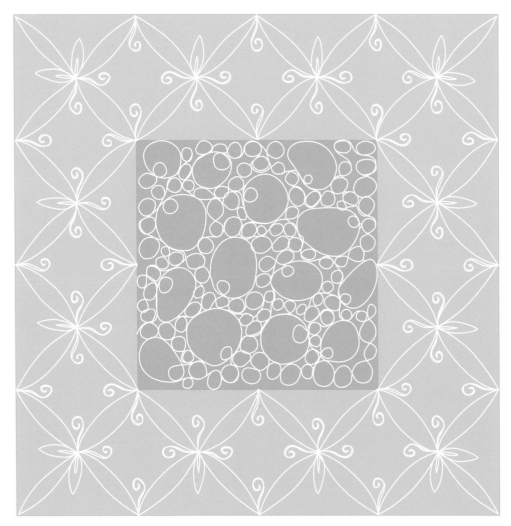

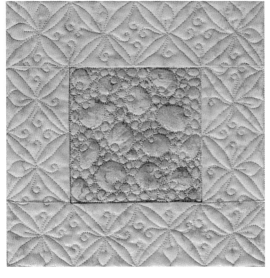

Refer to Connecting Loops (page 42) and Bubble Design (page 92) for stitching guidance.

Block 1: Waves

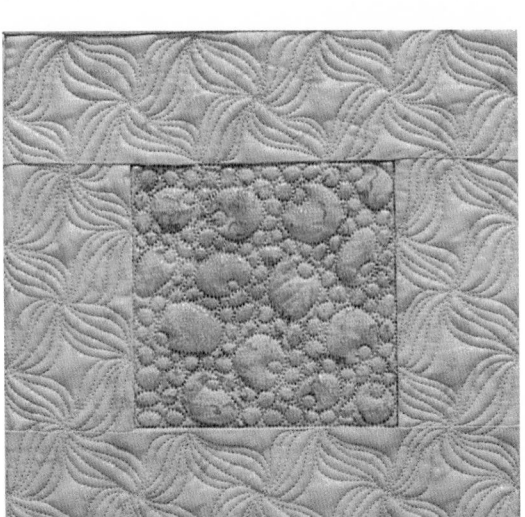

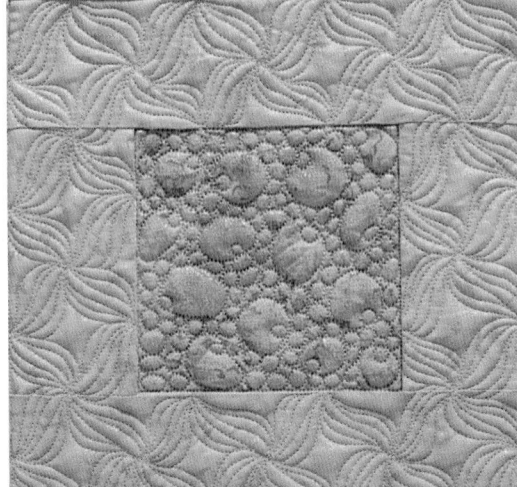

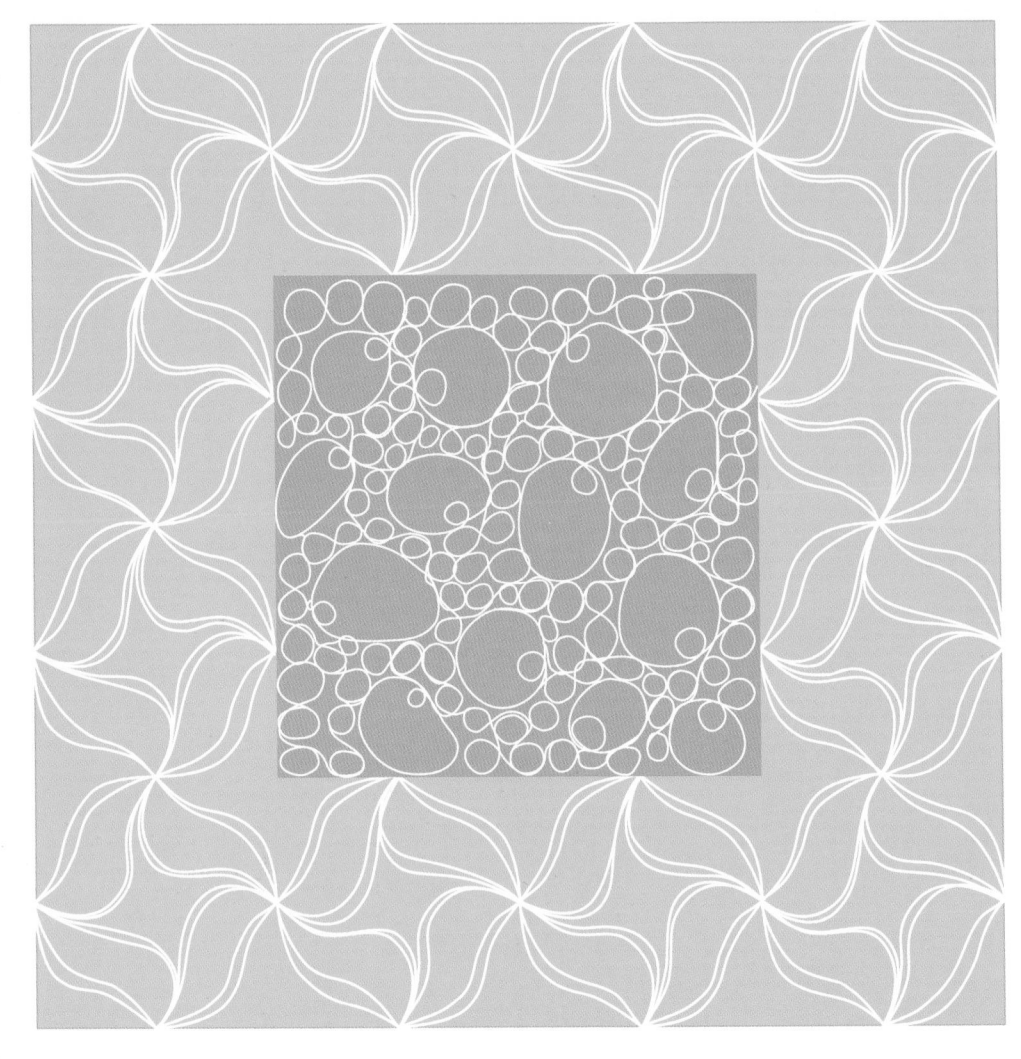

Refer to Connecting Waves (page 38) and Bubble Design (page 92) for stitching guidance.

Block 2: Brackets with Spikes

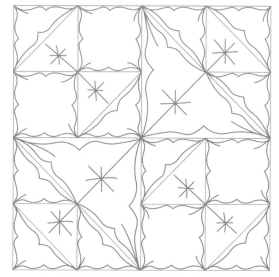

Refer to Snowflake (page 28) and Connecting Brackets with Spikes (page 62) for stitching guidance.

Note

Notice that I only used one spike, rather than two, for this design.

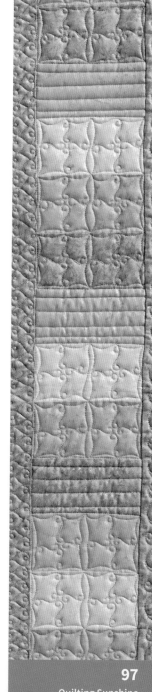

Block 2: Loops

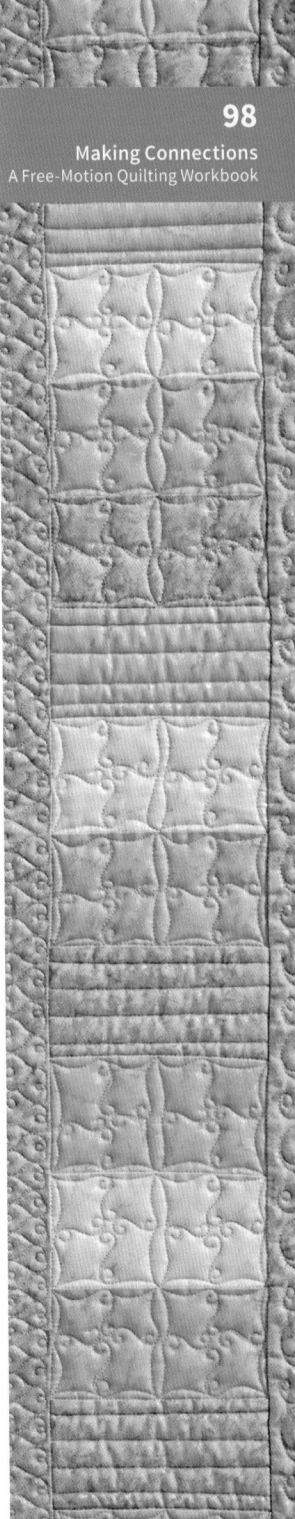

Refer to Connecting Loops (page 42) and Feather Plume (page 77) for stitching guidance.

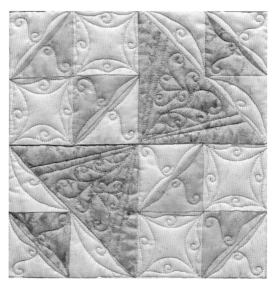

Refer to Connecting Curl 2 (page 50), Connecting Double Curls (page 54), and Feather Path (page 75) for stitching guidance.

Note

The two large blue triangles need to be stitched-in-the-ditch in order to travel around the block. The red dashed lines represent backtracking.

Block 2: Curl 1

Refer to Basic Connecting Designs (page 18) and Connecting Curl 1 (page 46) for stitching guidance.

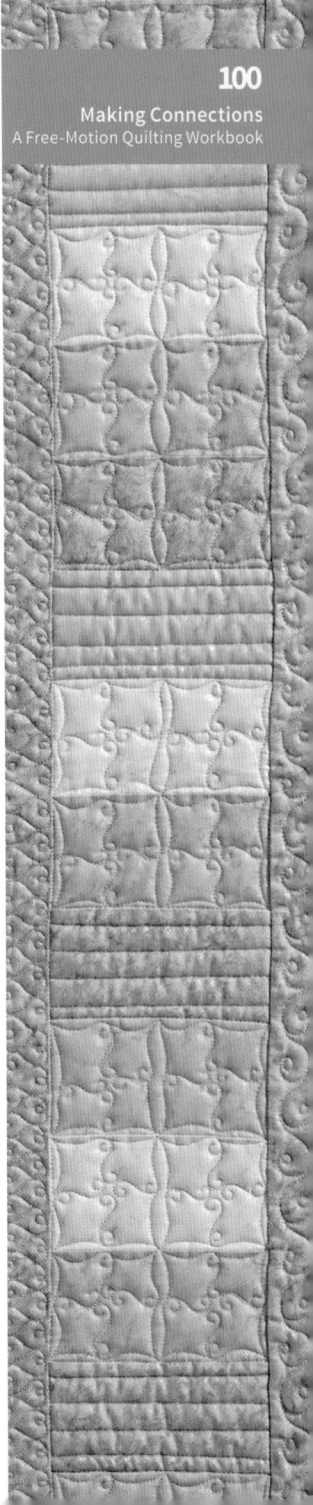

Refer to Basic Connecting Designs (page 18), Connecting Curves with Curls (page 34), and Feather Plume (page 77) for stitching guidance.

Refer to Connecting Curl 2 (page 50), Connecting Double Curls (page 54), and Feather Plume (page 77) for stitching guidance.

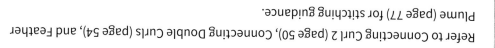

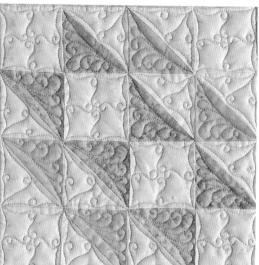

Block 3: Double Curls

Block 3: Curls with Leaves

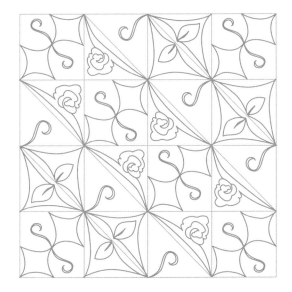

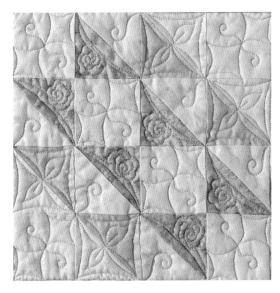

Refer to Connecting Curves with Leaves (page 30) and Connecting Curves with Curls (page 34) for stitching guidance.

Block 3: Loops and Petals

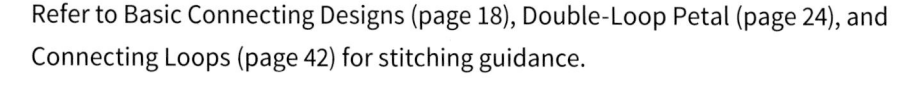

Refer to Basic Connecting Designs (page 18), Double-Loop Petal (page 24), and Connecting Loops (page 42) for stitching guidance.

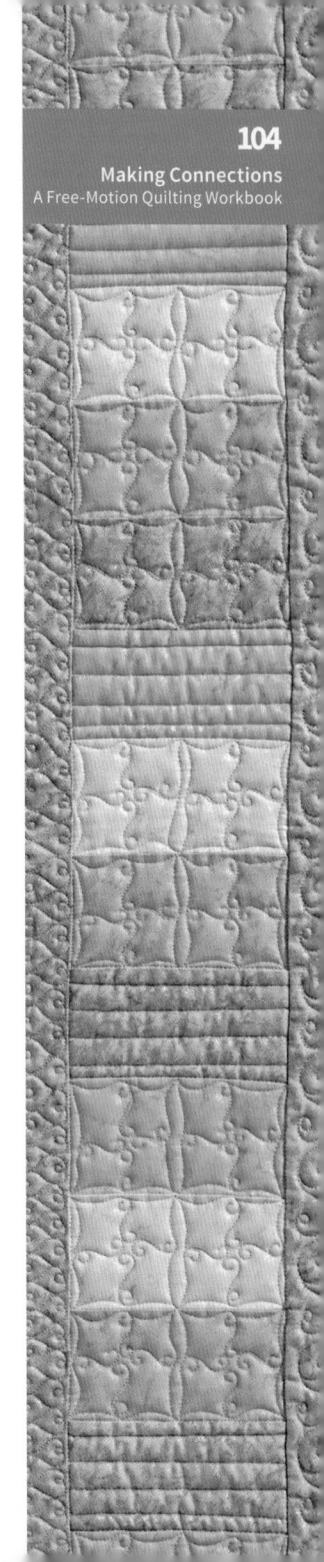

Triangles 1 and 2: Waves and Curl 2

Refer to Connecting Waves (page 38) for stitching guidance.

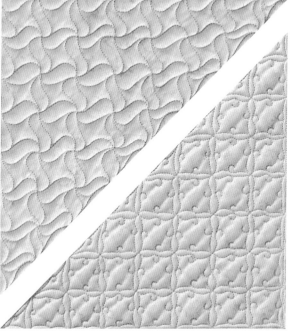

Refer to Connecting Curl 2 (page 50) for stitching guidance.

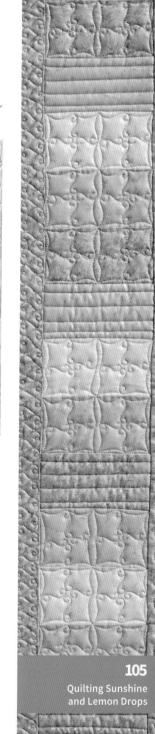

Triangles 3 and 4: Curves with Spikes and Curl 1

Refer to Connecting Curves with Spikes (page 26) for stitching guidance.

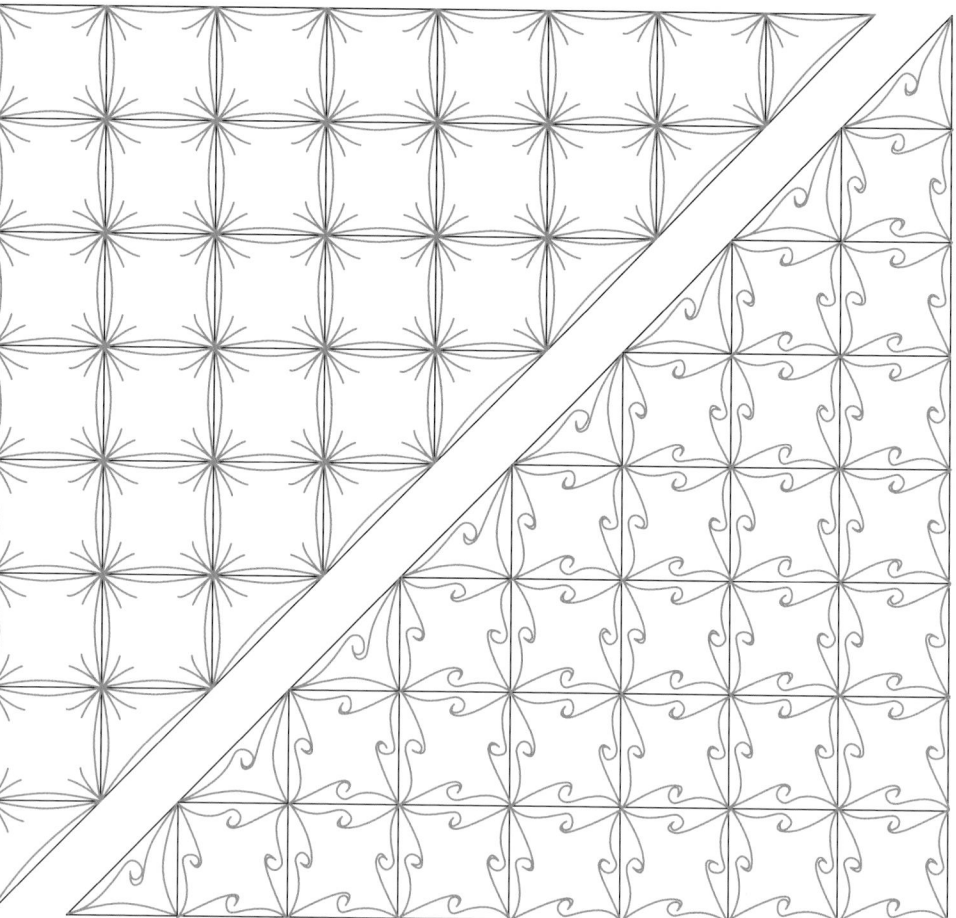

Refer to Connecting Curl 1 (page 46) for stitching guidance.

Triangles 5 and 6: Brackets and Loops

Refer to Connecting Brackets (page 58) for stitching guidance.

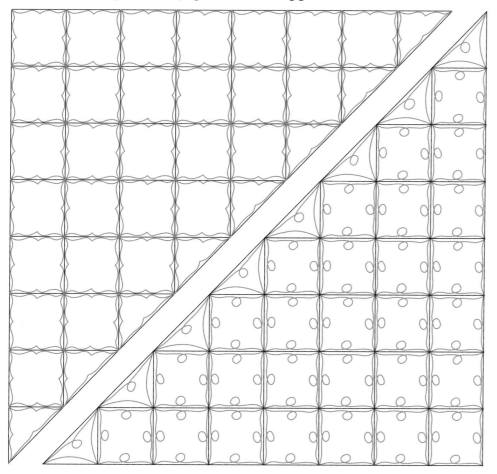

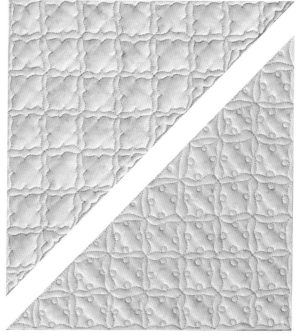

Refer to Connecting Loops (page 42) for stitching guidance.

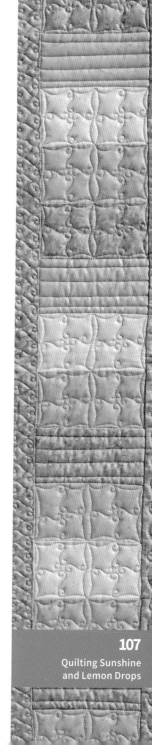

Triangles 7 and 8: Curves with Petals and Curves with Curls

Refer to Connecting Curves with Petals (page 22) for stitching guidance.

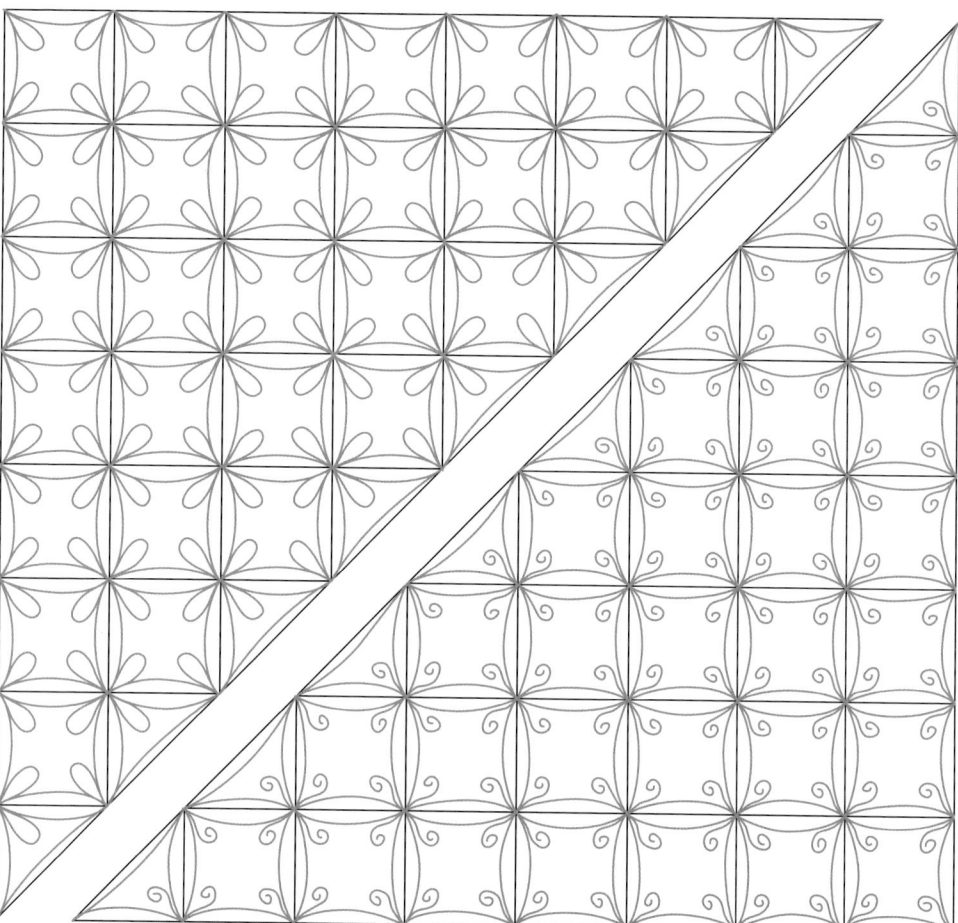

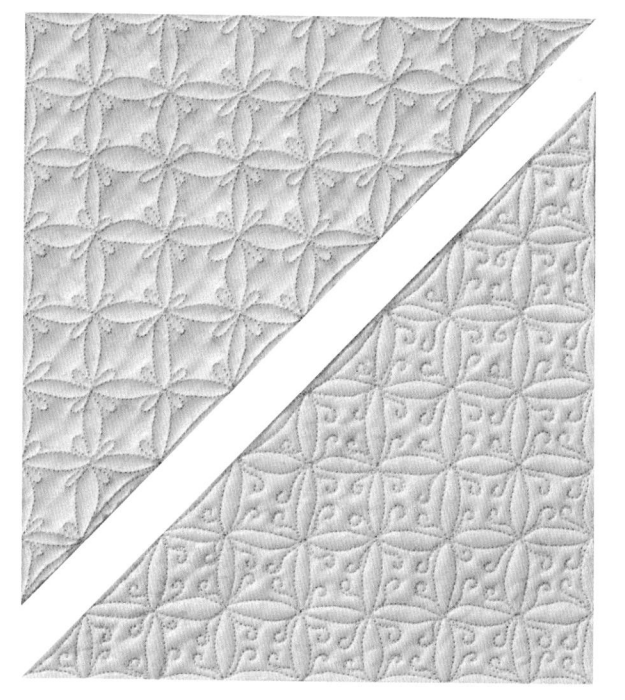

Refer to Connecting Curves with Curls (page 34) for stitching guidance.

Corner Triangles

Refer to Basic Connecting Designs (page 18) and Connecting Curl 2 (page 50) for stitching guidance.

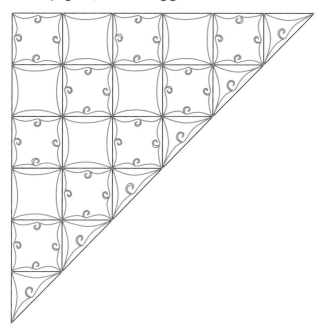

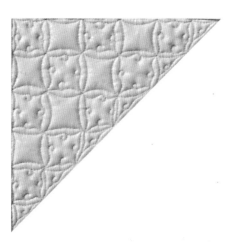

Border Corner Squares

Refer to Basic Connecting Designs (page 18), Connecting Double Curls (page 54), and Feather Plumes (page 77) for stitching guidance.

About the Author

Dorie Hruska is an award-winning longarm quilter, teacher, and author. She began her quilt obsession at the age of fifteen, when she pieced and quilted her first quilt, a Lone Star pattern. In 2002, she began her professional longarm quilting business just three weeks after purchasing her first quilting machine. In addition to winning numerous ribbons for her machine quilting, Dorie's work has been featured on the cover of a magazine, in a wall calendar, and in other authors' books. In 2006, after discovering a love for hexagons, she started designing patterns and teaching classes on her method of hand basting and piecing hexagon designs. Her quilt, *Flourishing Garden*, featuring layered hexagons, has won multiple awards. In addition to giving trunk shows and teaching classes on machine quilting and English paper piecing hexagons, Dorie enjoys filling her time quilting for others on her APQS long-arm quilting machine. Dorie lives in Highlandville, Missouri, with her husband and two teenage children.

Want even
more creative
content?

MENU ☰

STUDIO

C&T PUBLISHING Your Home for Creative Quilting & Sewing

HAND PRINTING

Print on Almost Anything!

Get some
@ in-spiration

GET INSPIRED

GARMENT SEWING LOOKBOOK 2016

Make it,
snap it,
share it
using
#ctpublishing